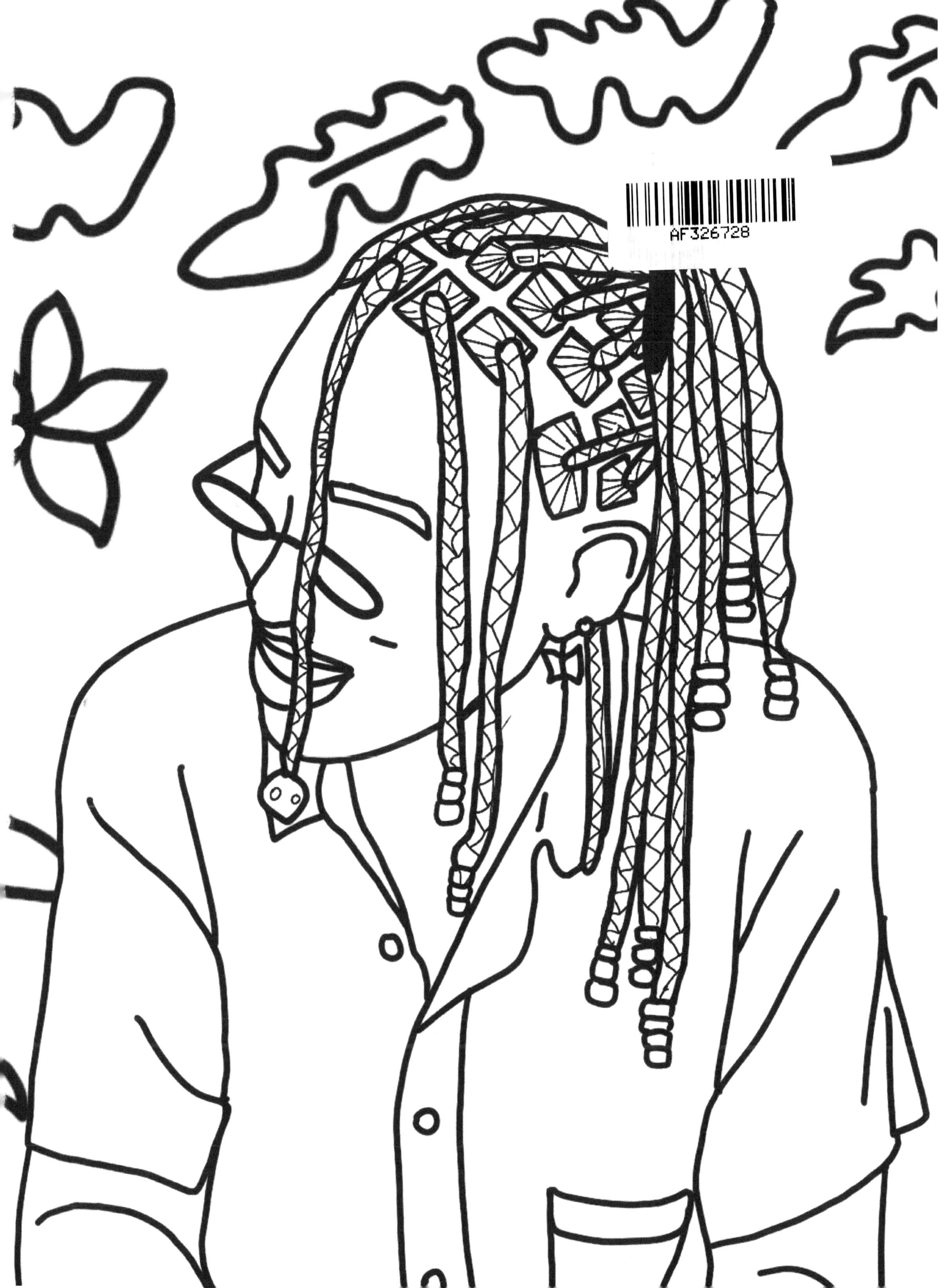
AF326728

Published by

Revolutionary Hearts Industries

Illustrated by Naomi Winston

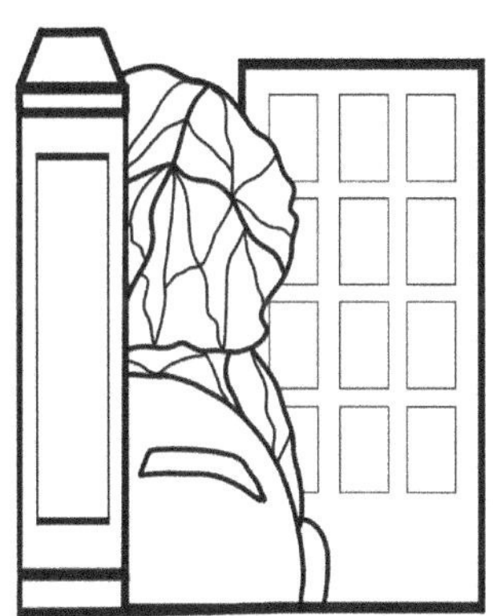

To someone with a beautiful curly and kinky crown,

Loving yourself can come in many forms, but one is protecting your crown. A crown is not only a physical piece of gold and silver adorned with jewels but also one that grows out of your head. There is a reason that your hair stretches out towards the sun, growing like a flower toward its rays. There is a reason that your hair stretches outwards as far and wide as you will allow it.

Your hair is your crown, so be protective of whom you let touch it. Your hair is your crown, so be proud of the way that it shines and grows. Just like a crown of silver and gold, your crown of curls and kinks deserves to be cared for just as intentionally.

Remember that you have the power to decorate, change, and customize your crown as much as you want because it is YOURS.

Your hair is beautiful. Your hair is powerful. Your hair is golden.

Love your hair, and remember that we, as the older Black community, will always work to help you nourish, showcase, and protect your crown. (Look up the Crown Act!)

Everything has a purpose, and you are everything.

LETTER FROM THE AUTHOR

SELF LOVE: CROWN EDITION

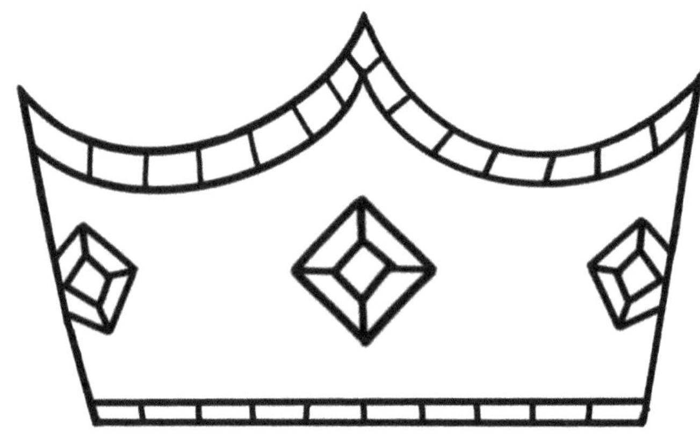

What does my crown look like?

Draw yourself with the way your hair looks now!

____

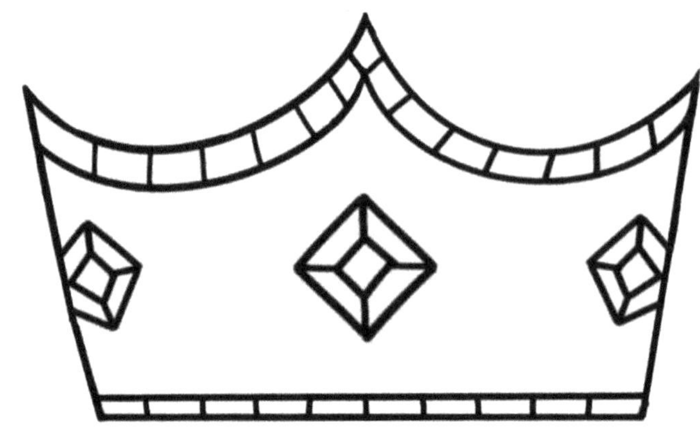

My crown is worthy of being loved, especially by me!

____

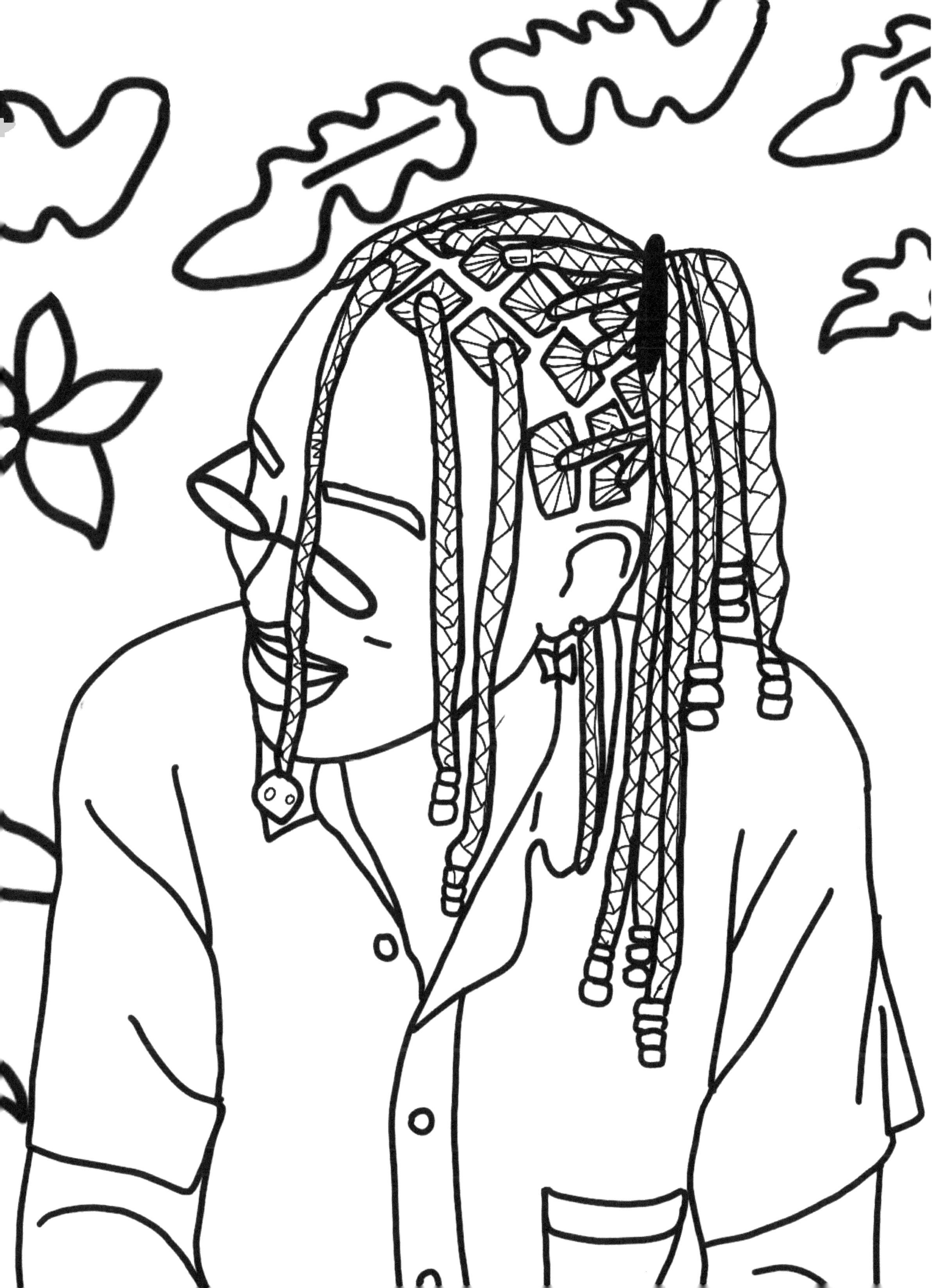

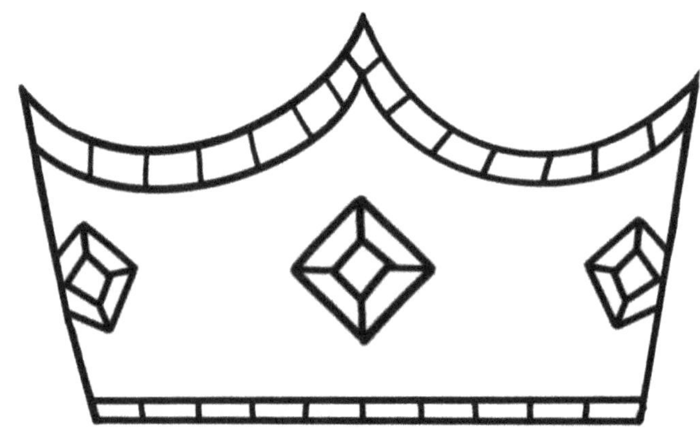

My beauty is not tied to how my hair looks or appears in certain spaces.

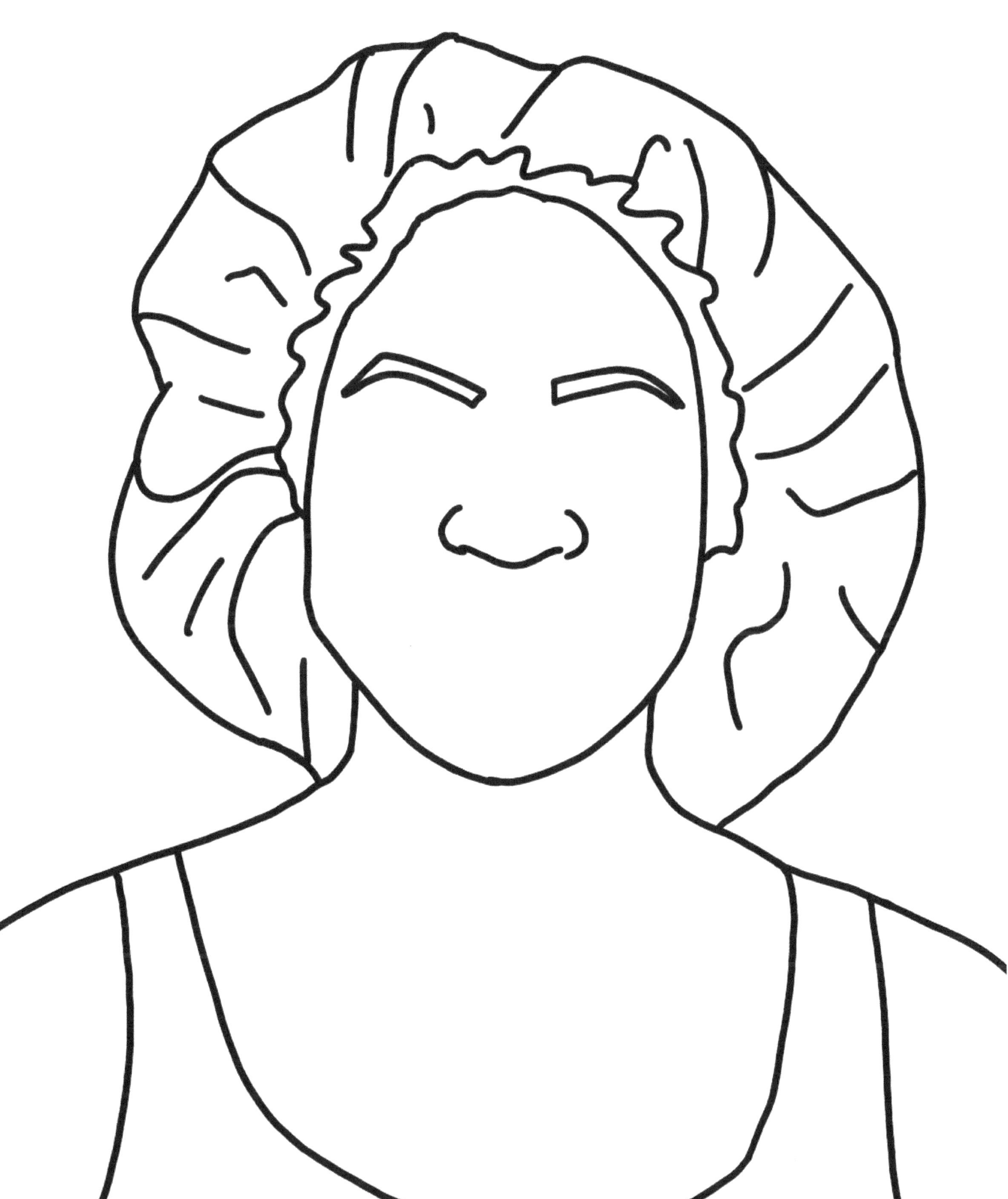

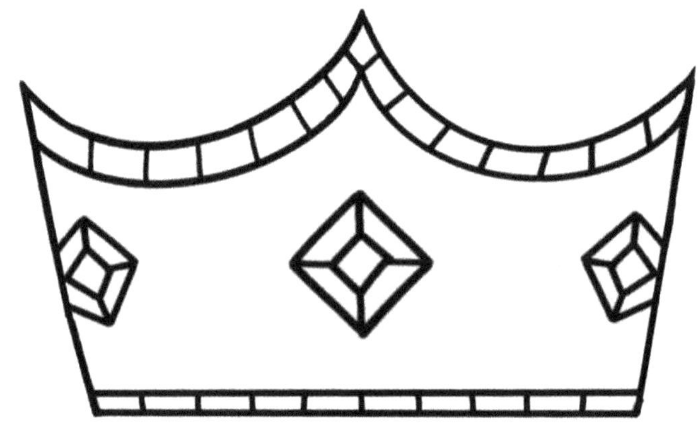

My natural hair is a professional style.

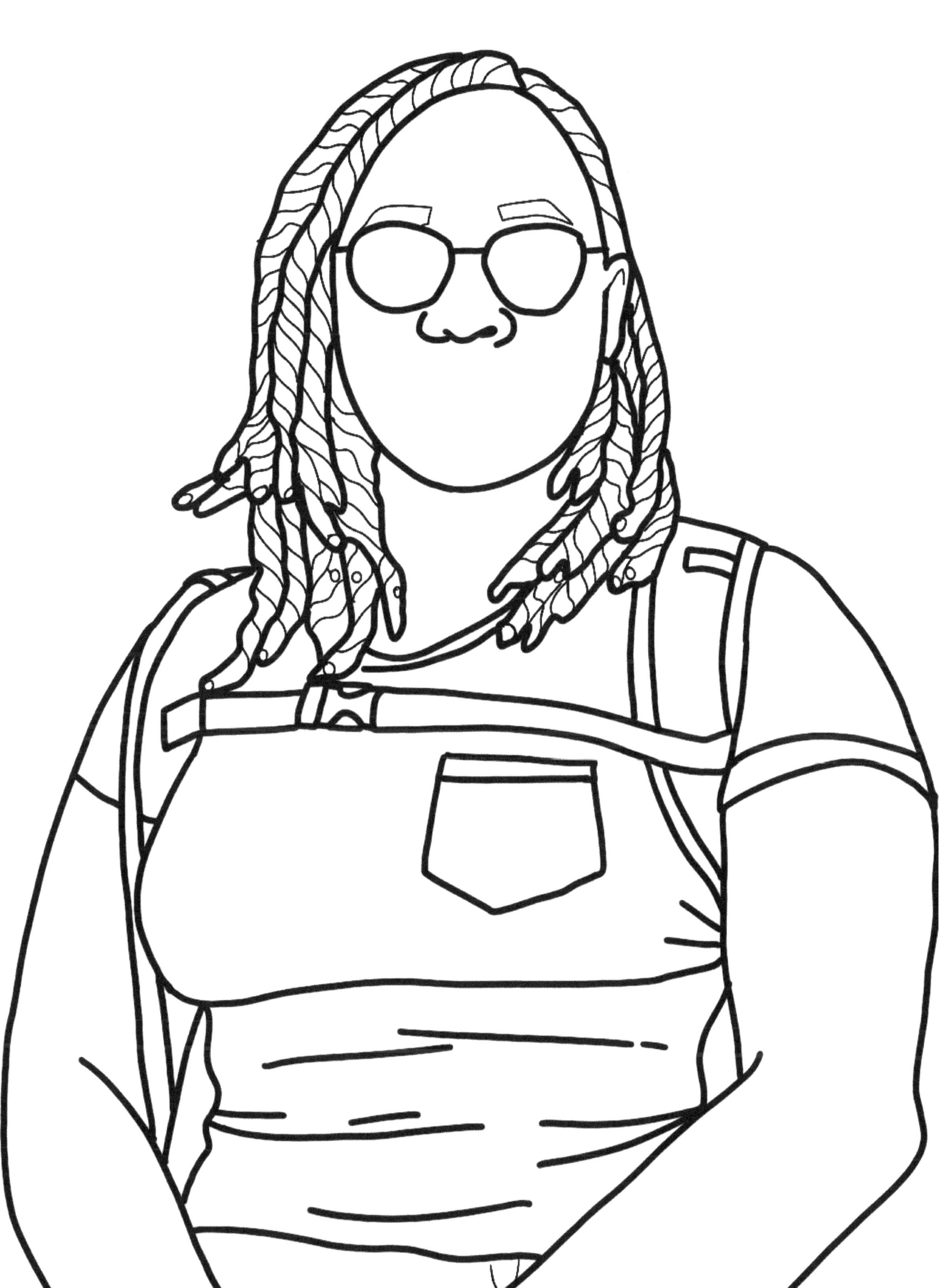

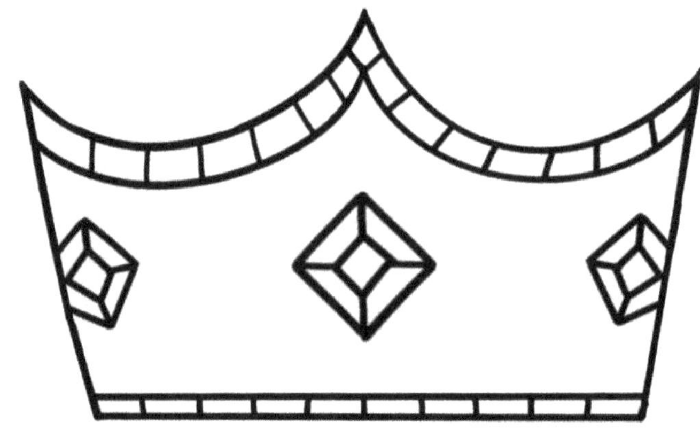

I deserve to like the way that I look.

____

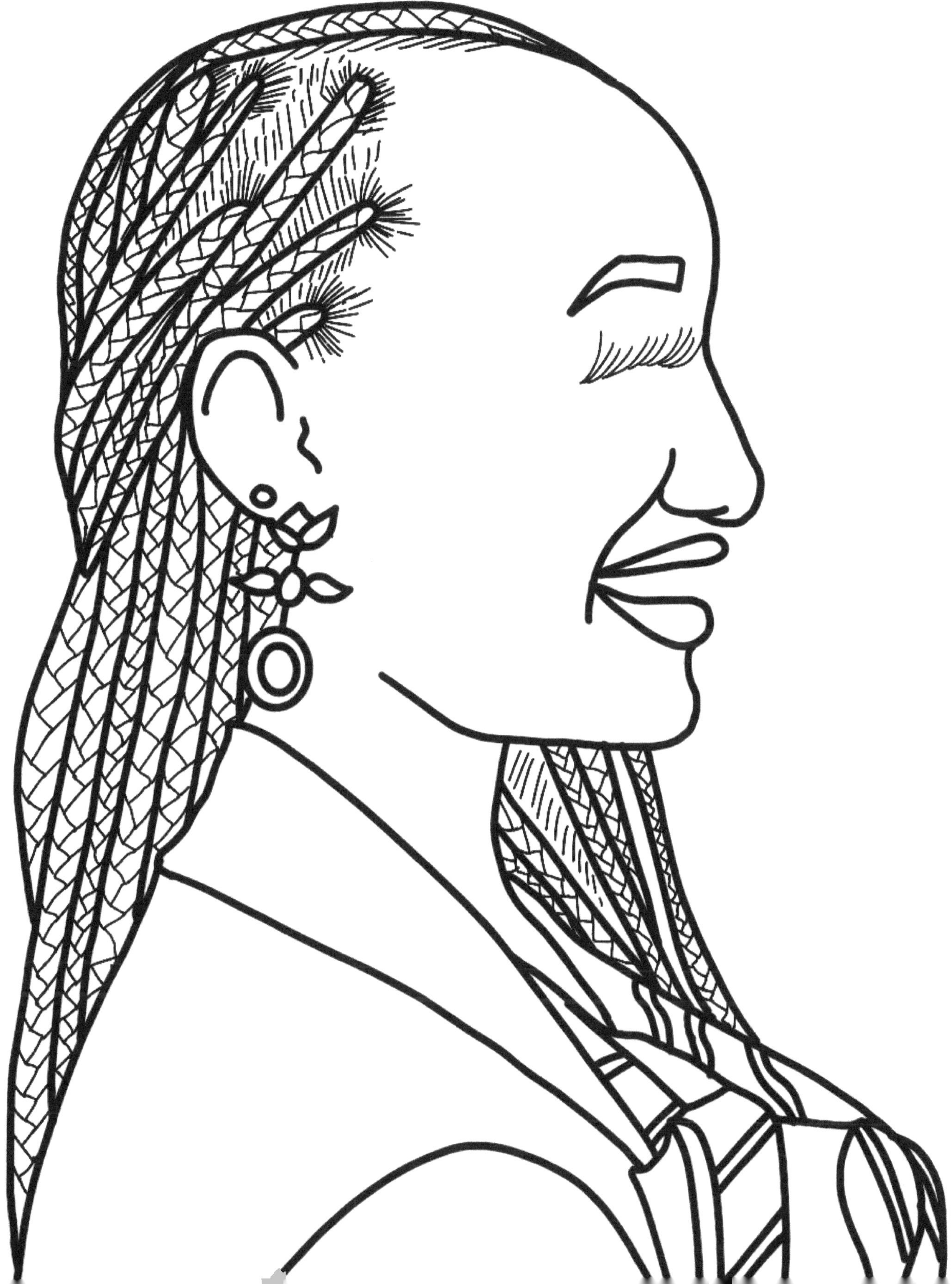

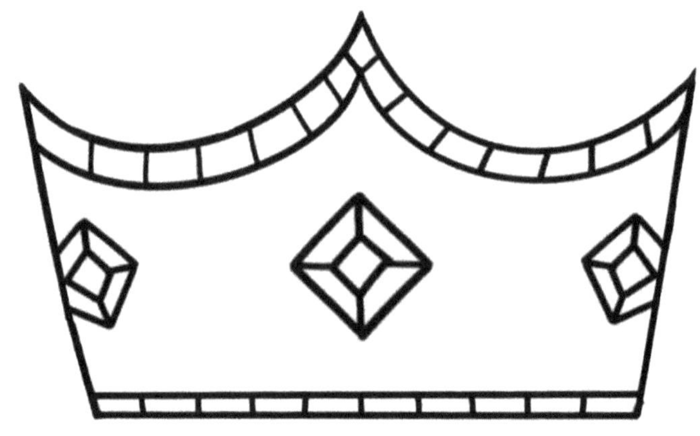

Hair grows back, so I don't need to be afraid to try something new!

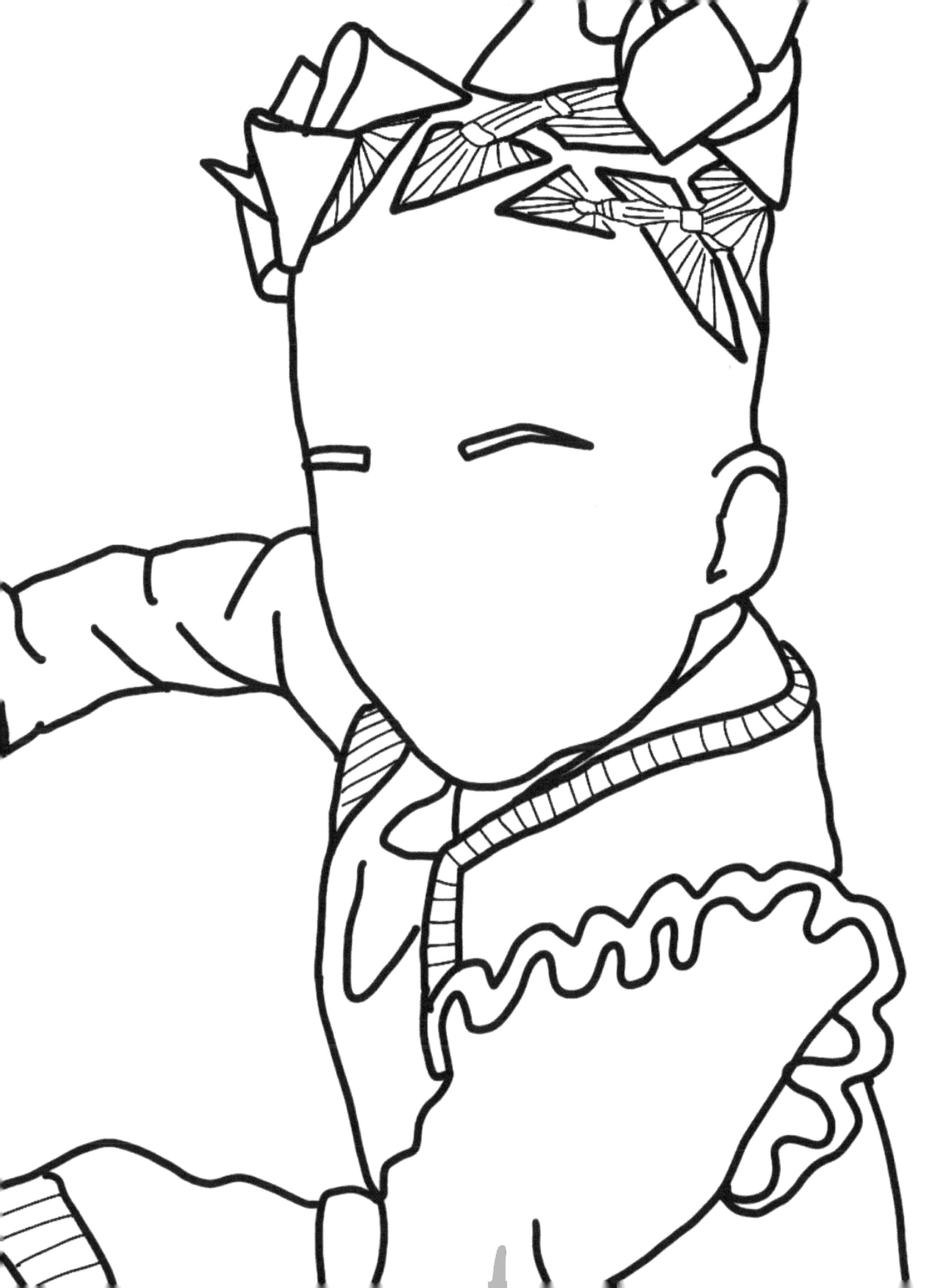

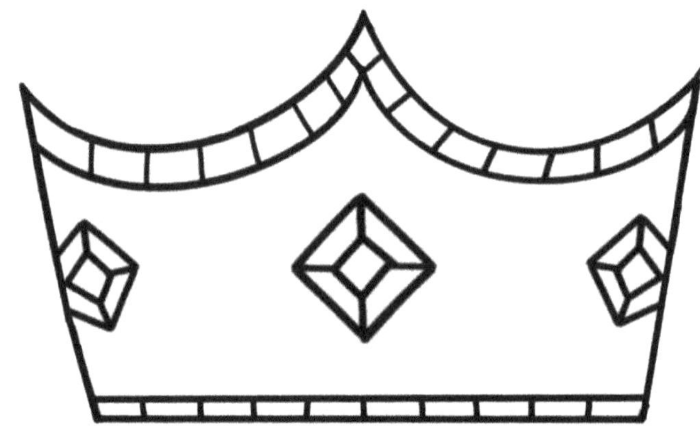

I remember wrapping my hair up at night so it looks like new!

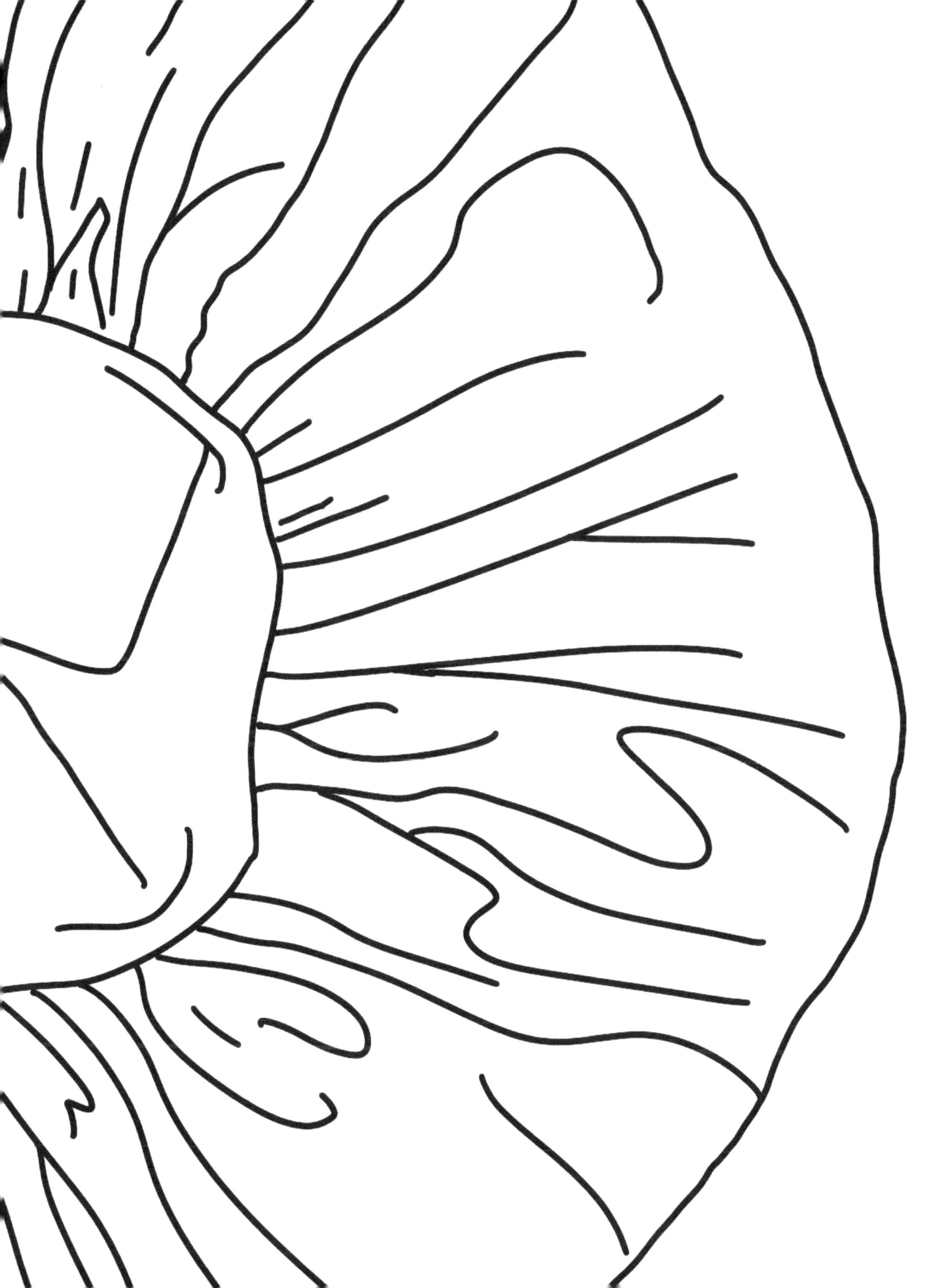

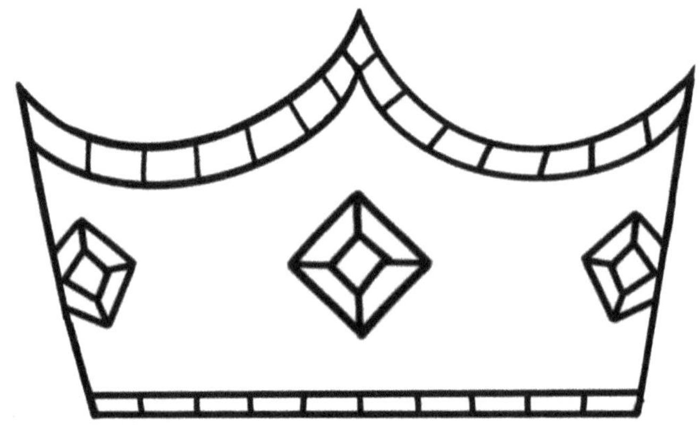

My hair is tied to a rich history of African ancestry.

____

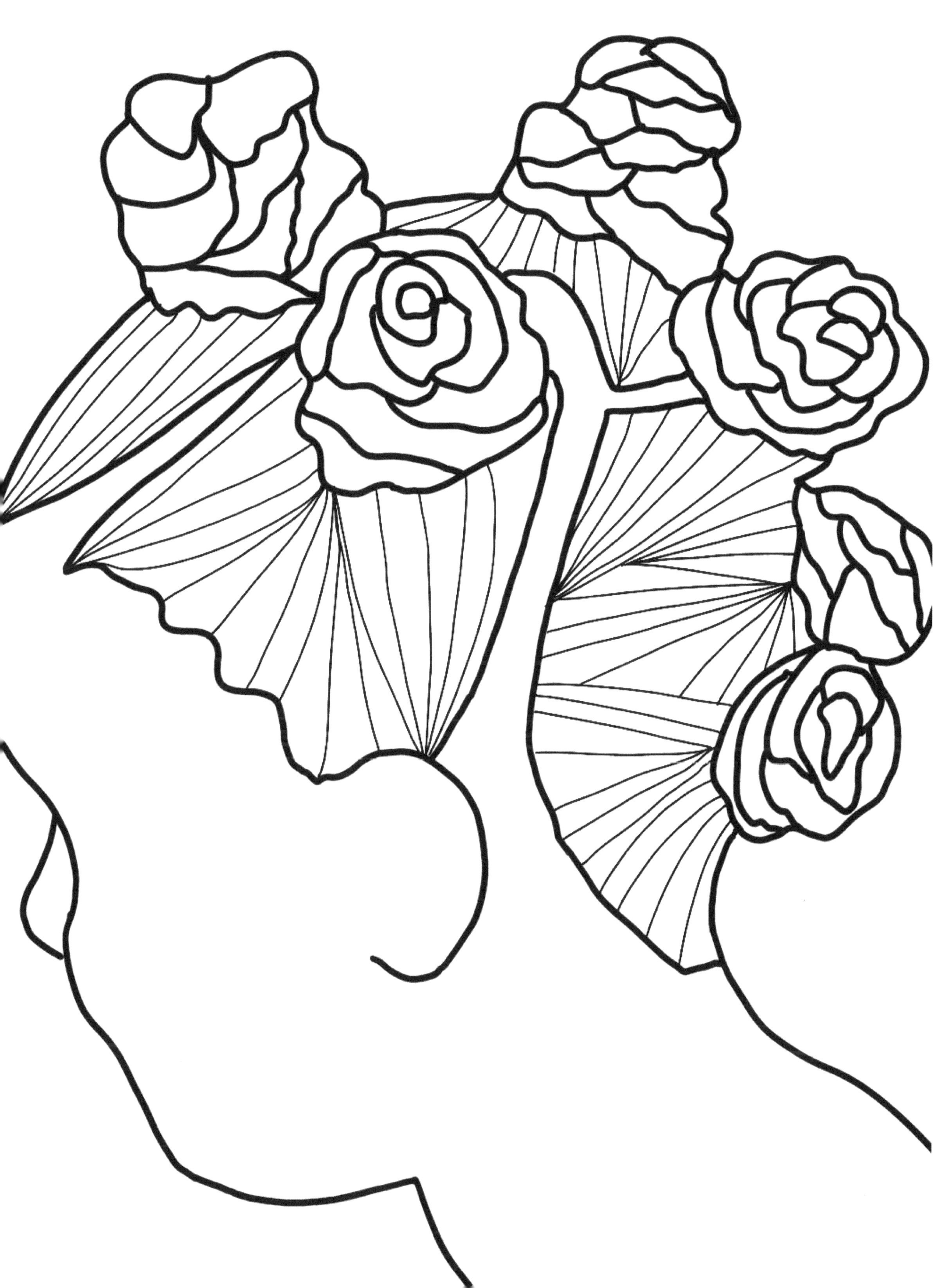

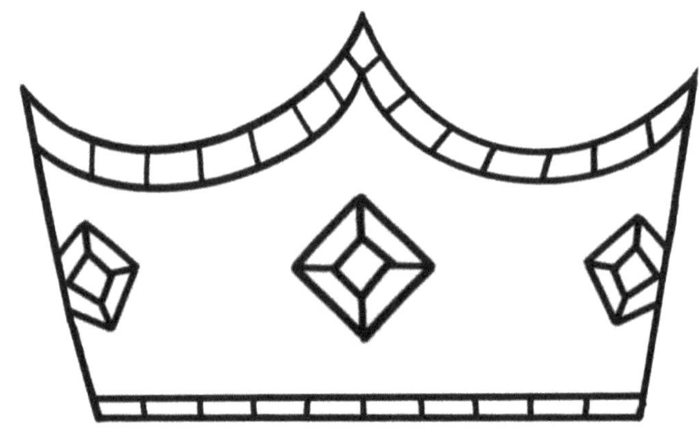

I am proud of the history that lies in the kinks, curls, and knots in my hair.

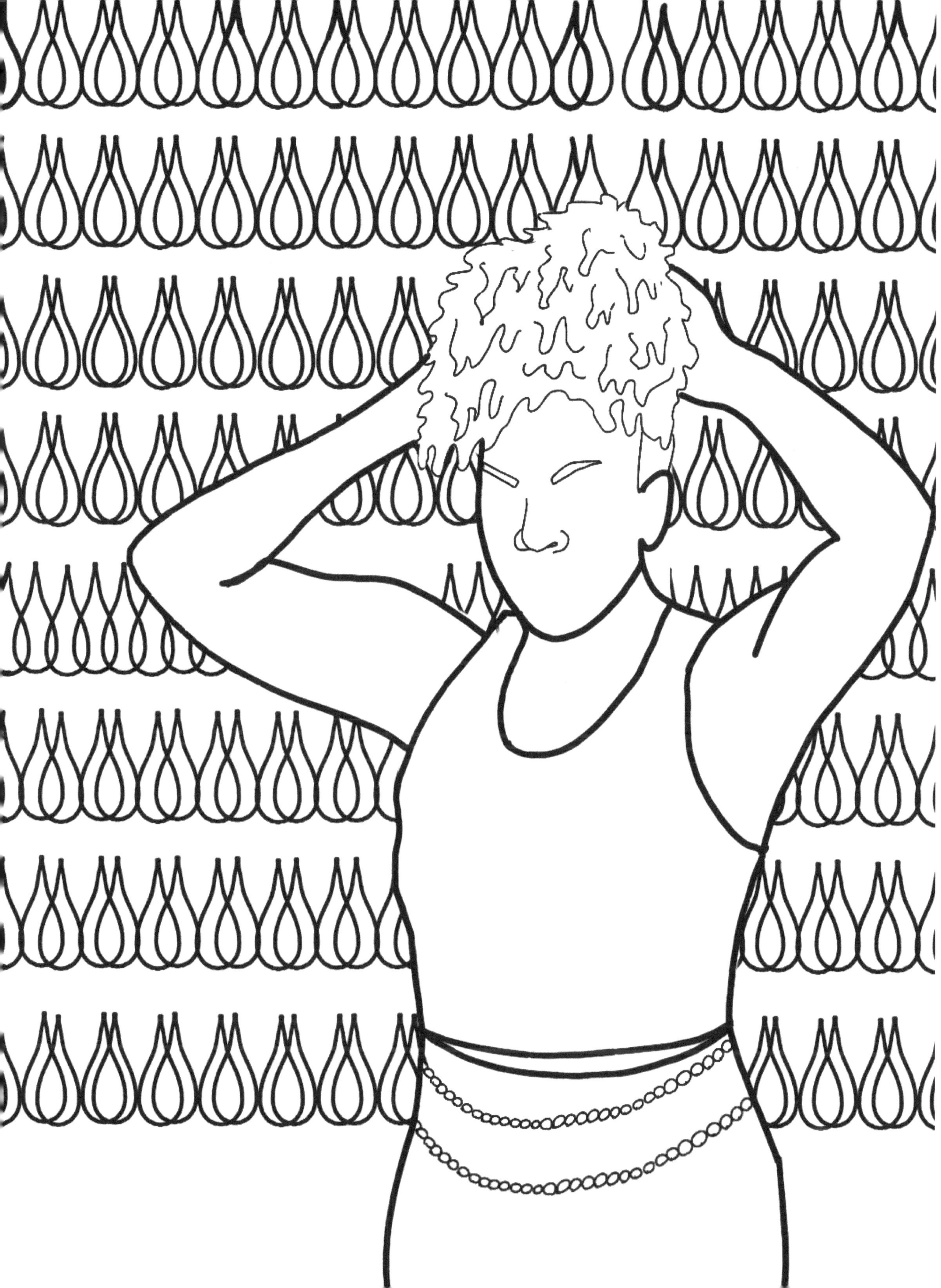

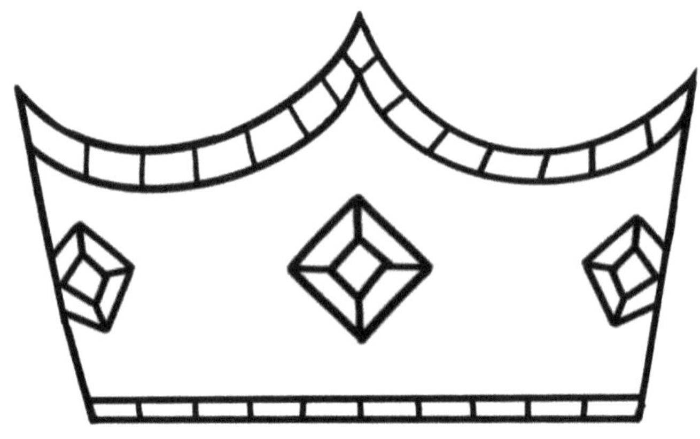

My hair is beautiful the way it is naturally.

____

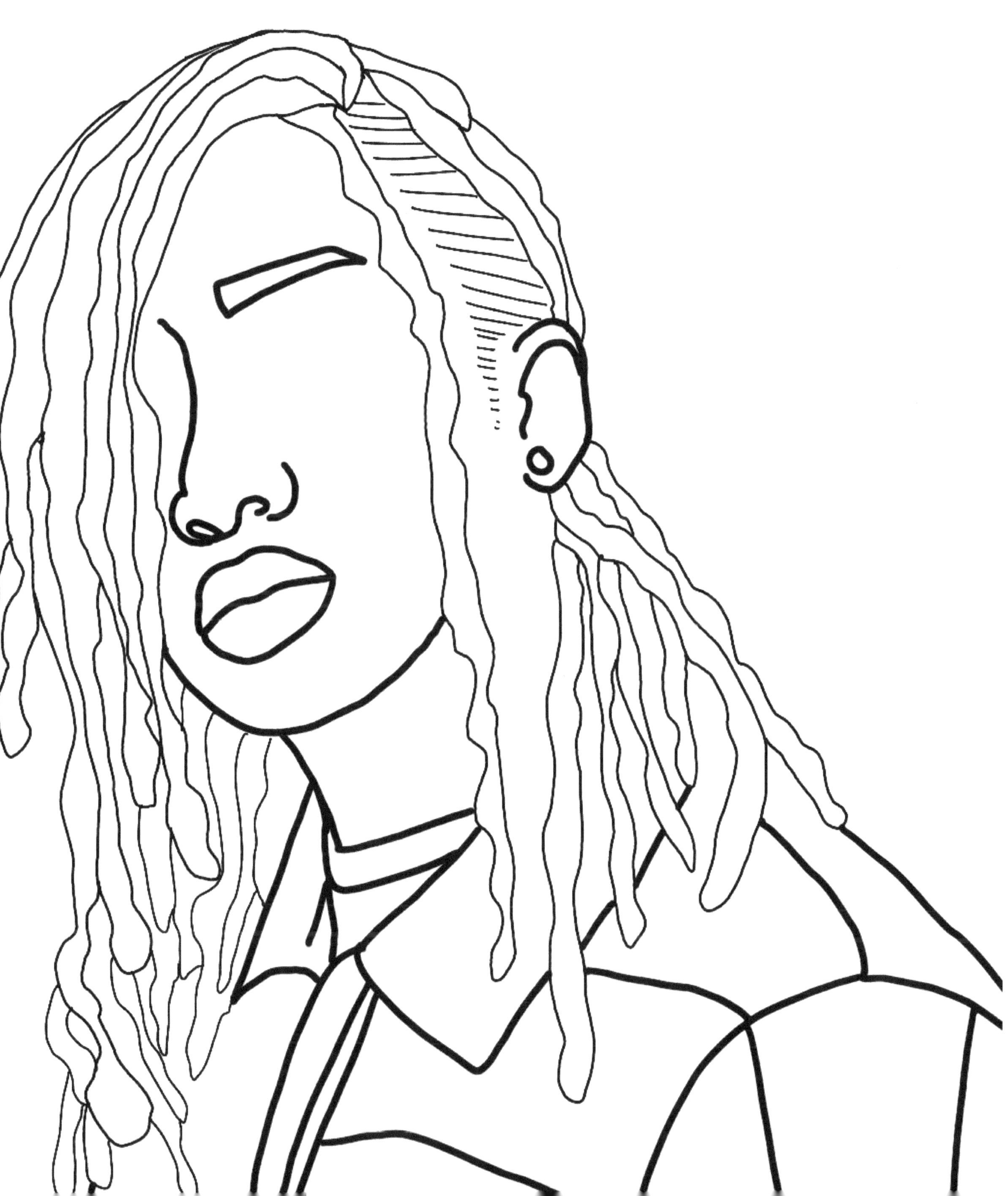

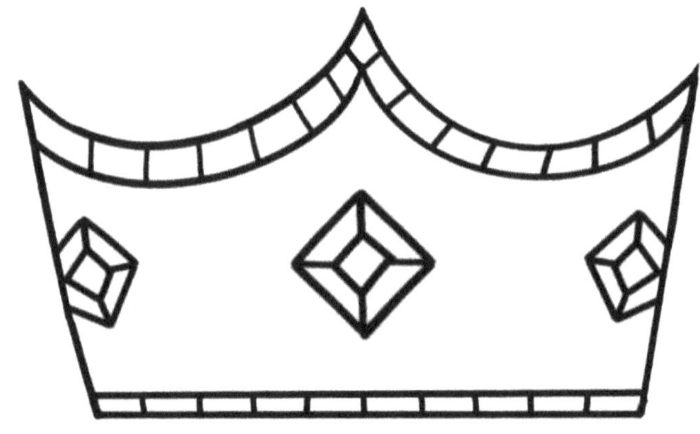

If I don't like the way that I look I have the power, resources, and autonomy to change that.

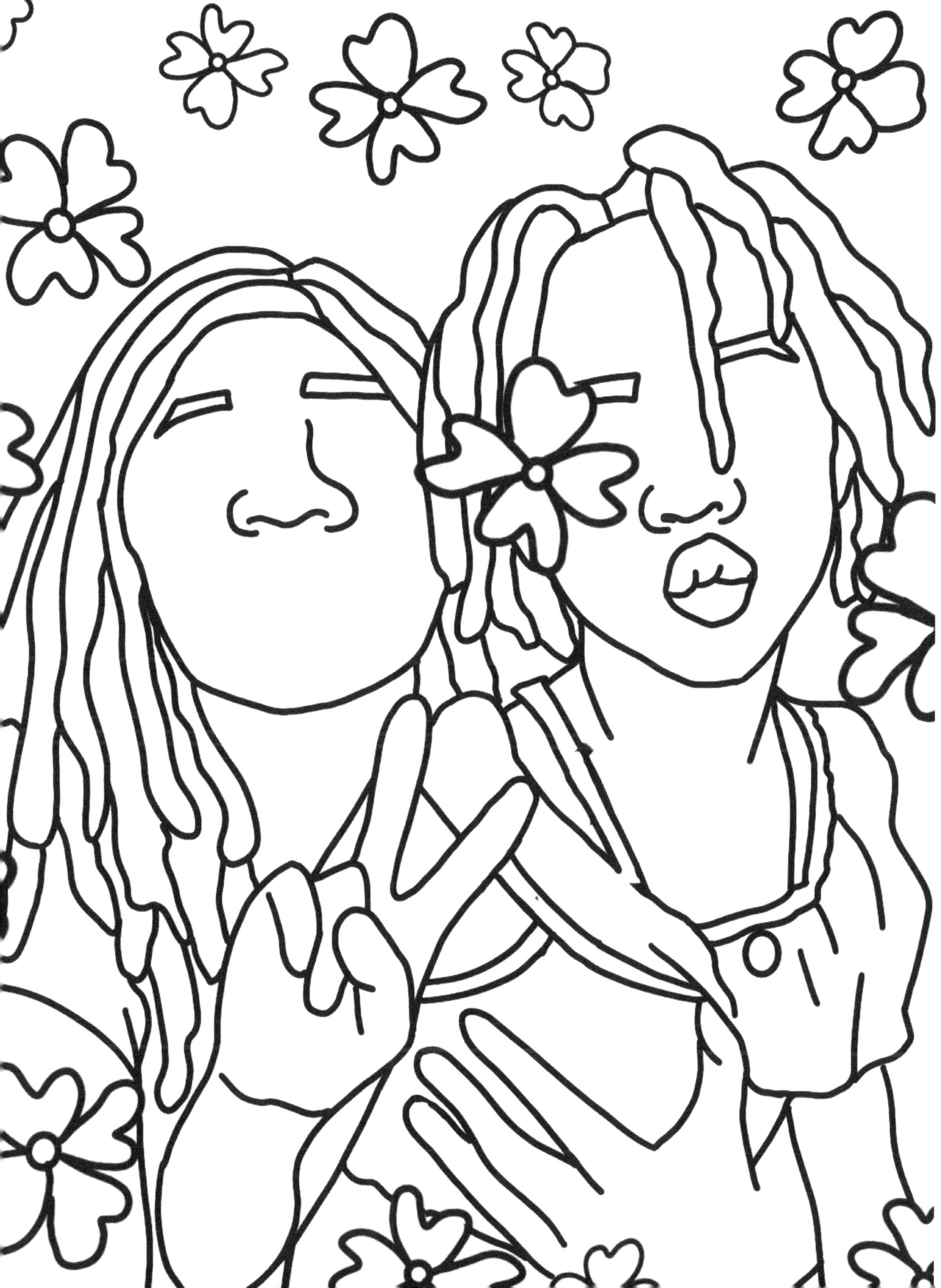

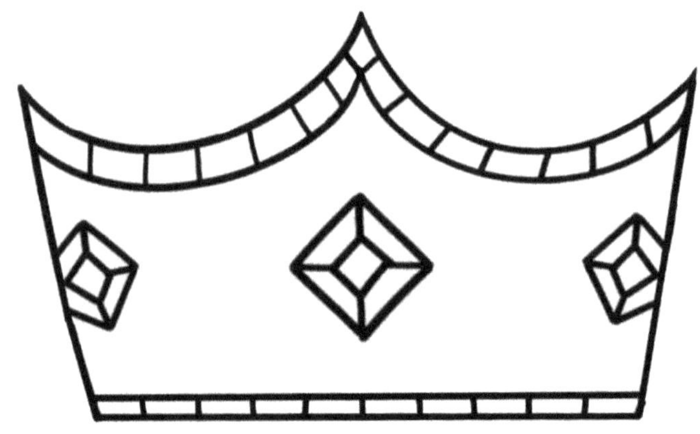

No one is allowed to touch my crown without my permission.

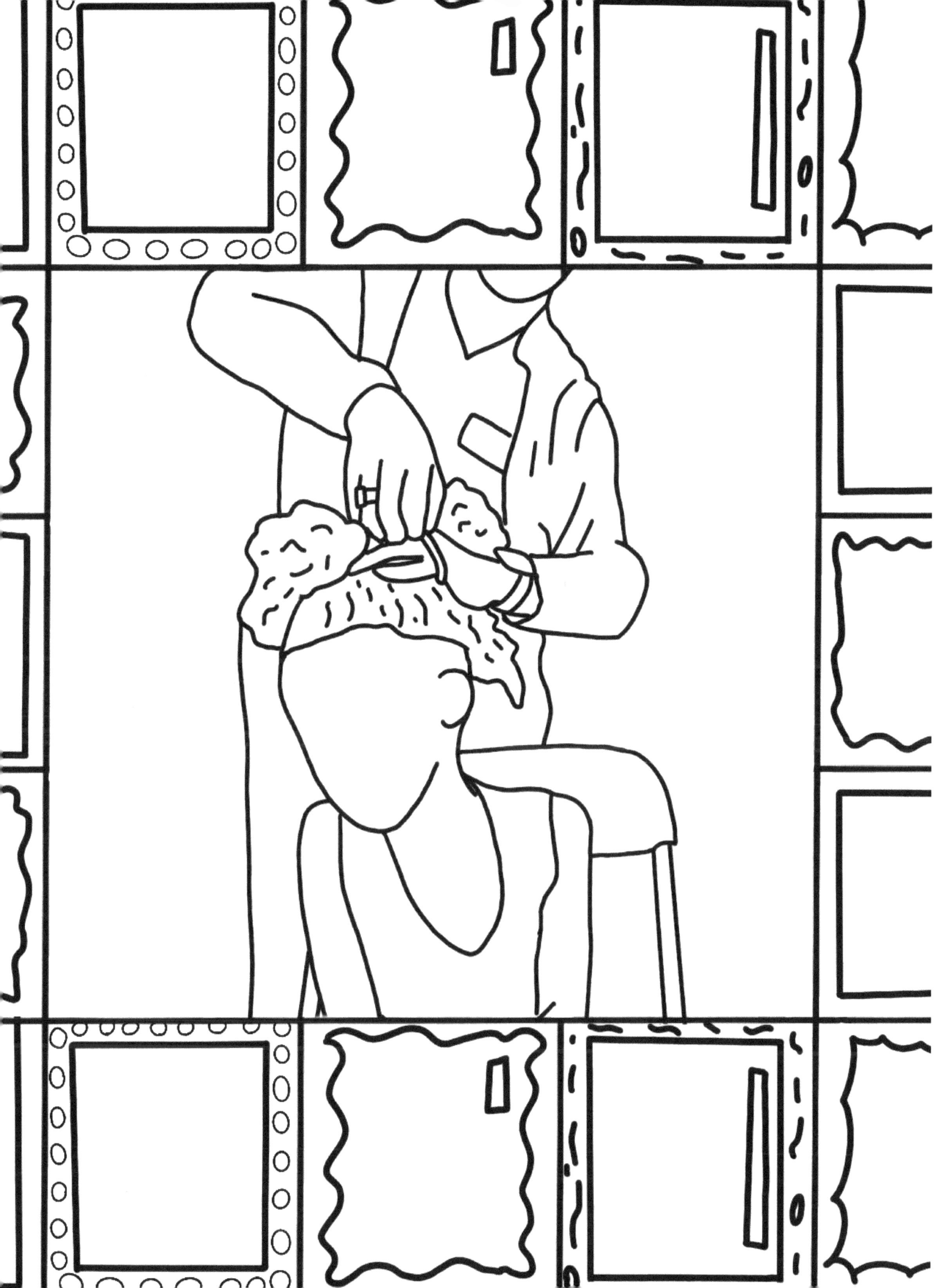

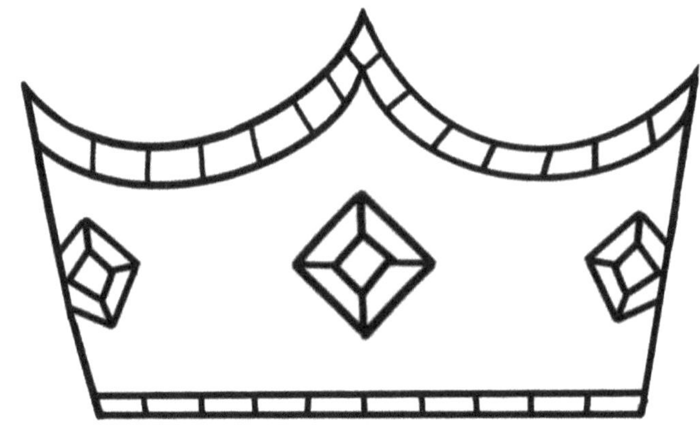

I will keep my hair moisturized and will make sure to comb my hair when it is wet to avoid breakage.

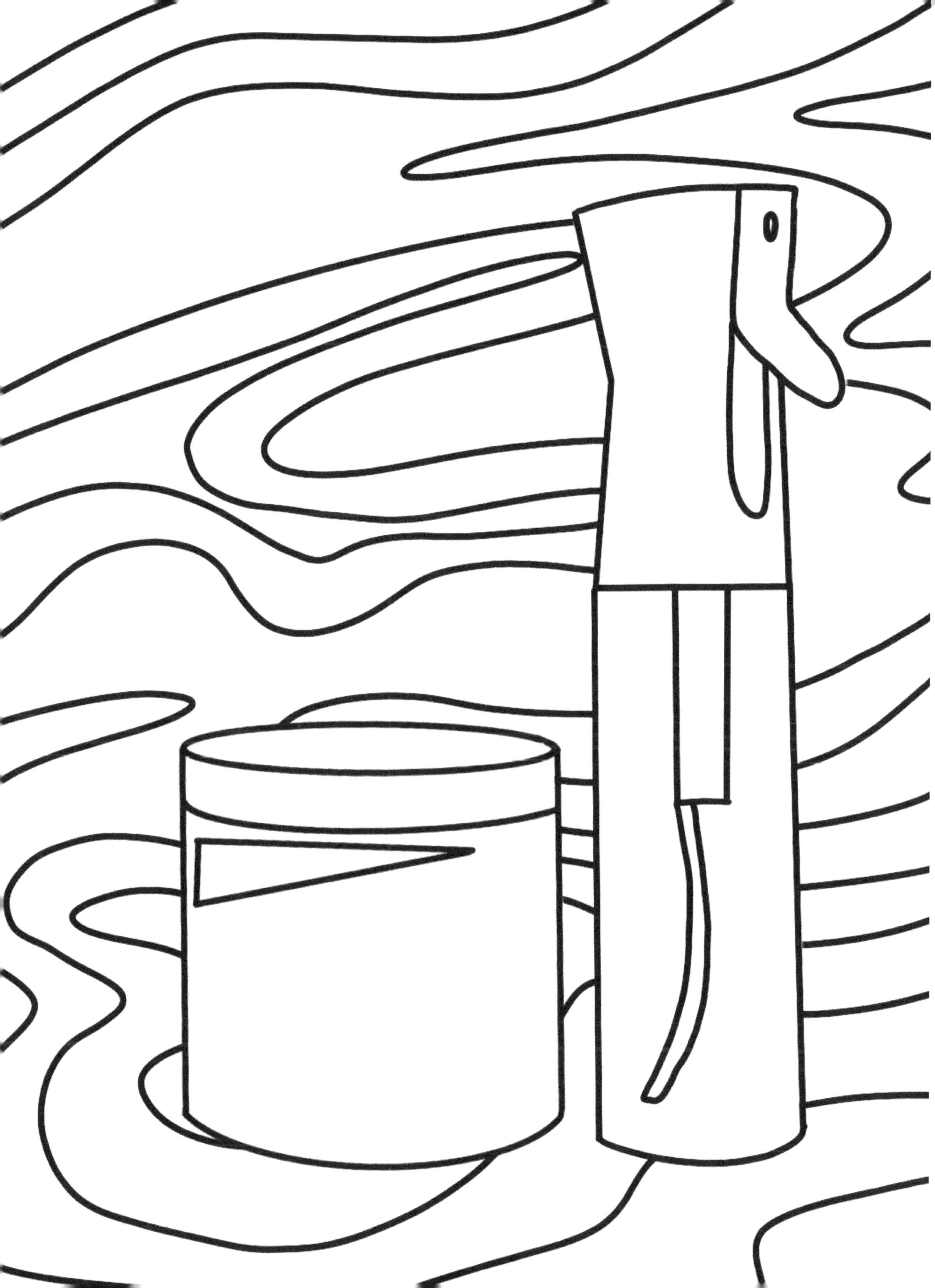

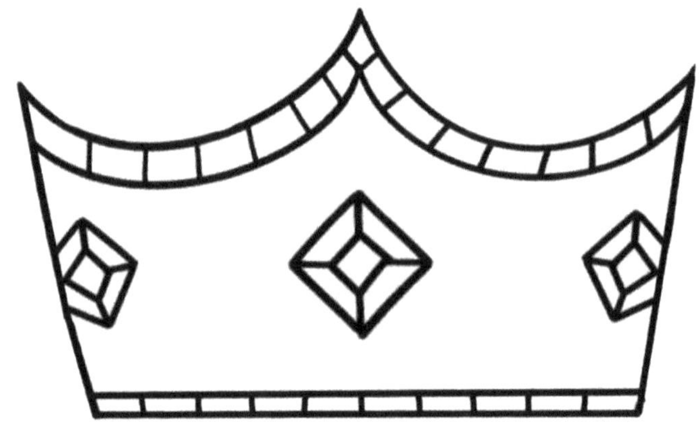

My crown is so beautiful that it can take shape in any way it is molded.

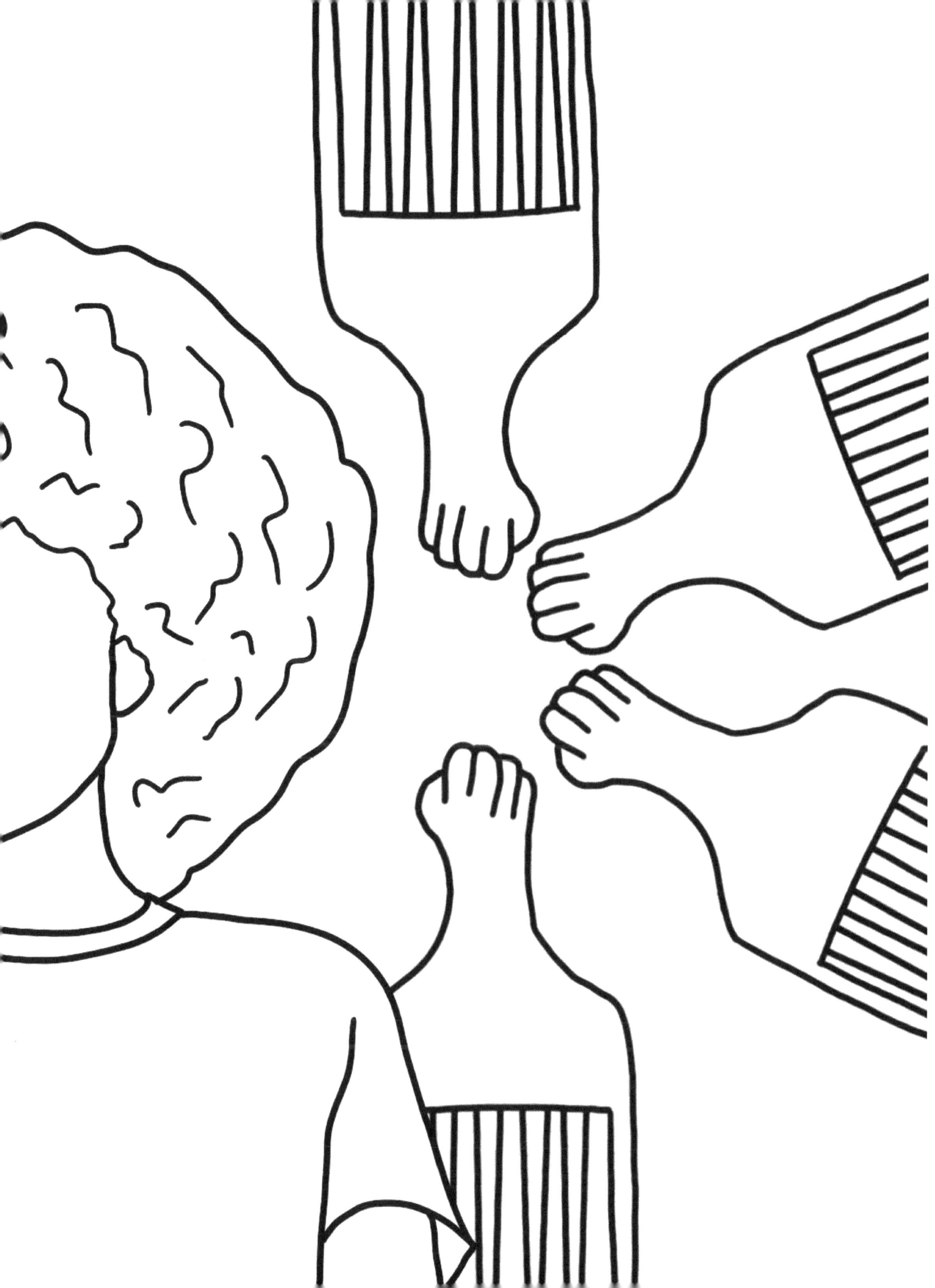

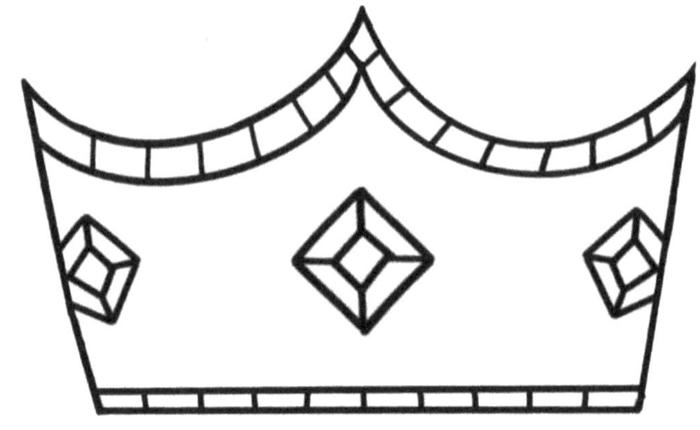

I love my hair. I love the way that I look. I love myself without ego but filled with confidence.

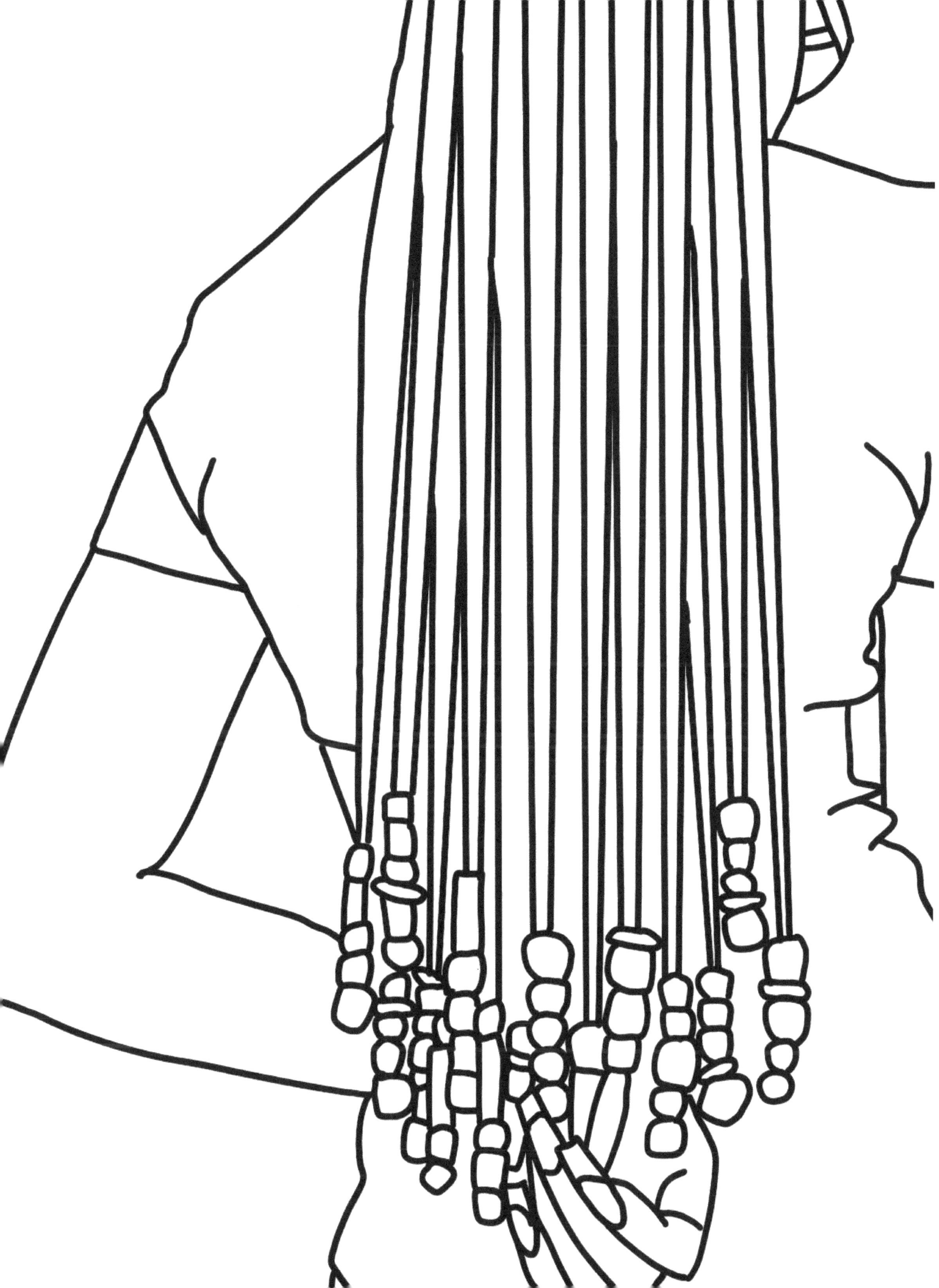

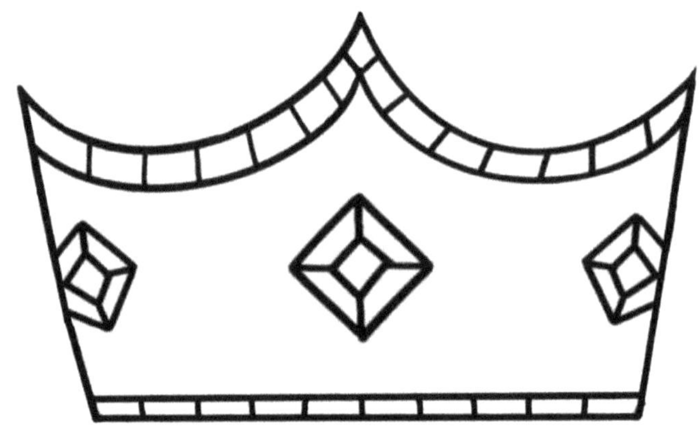

My hair is like clay, and I am the sculptor.

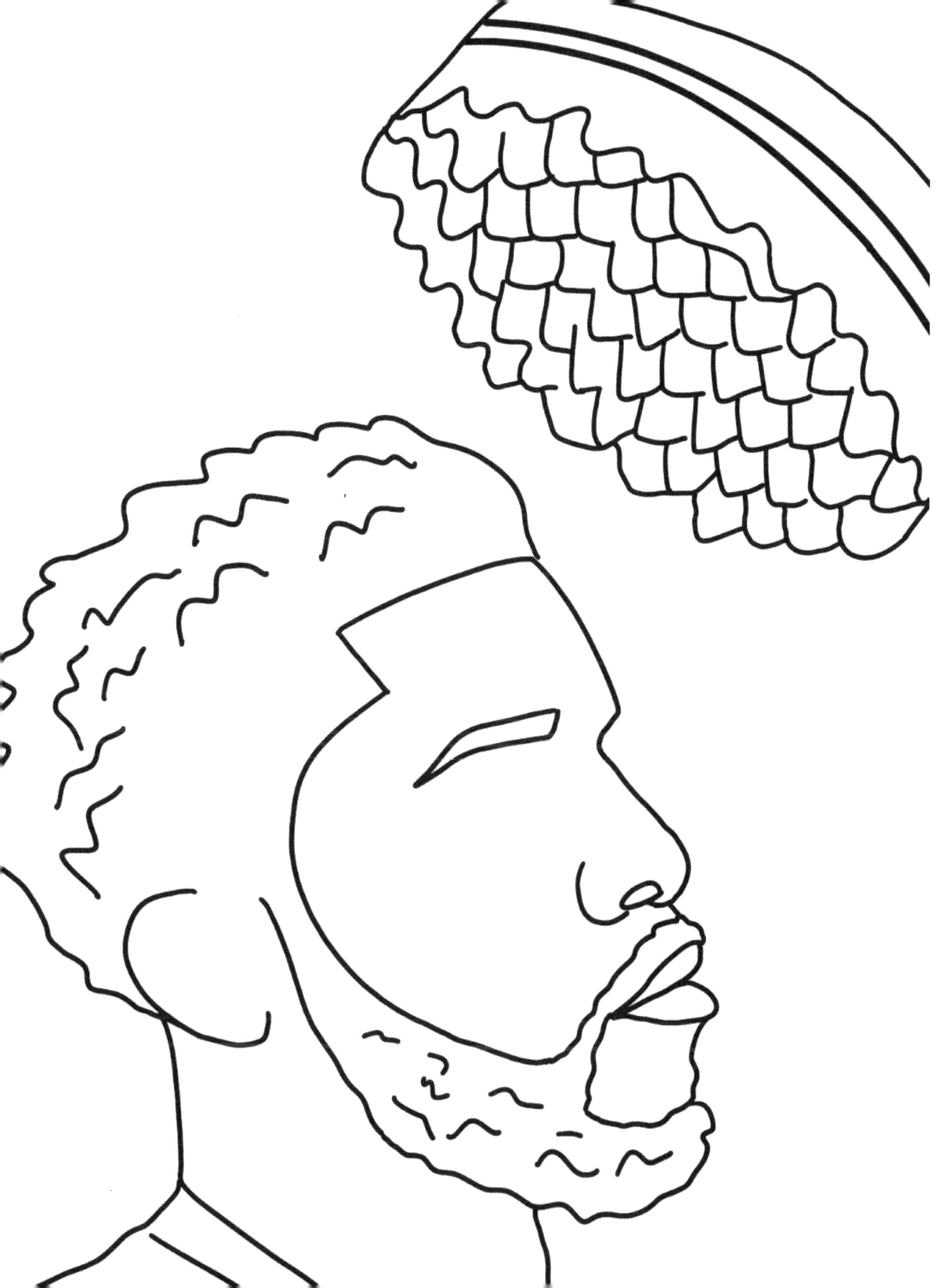

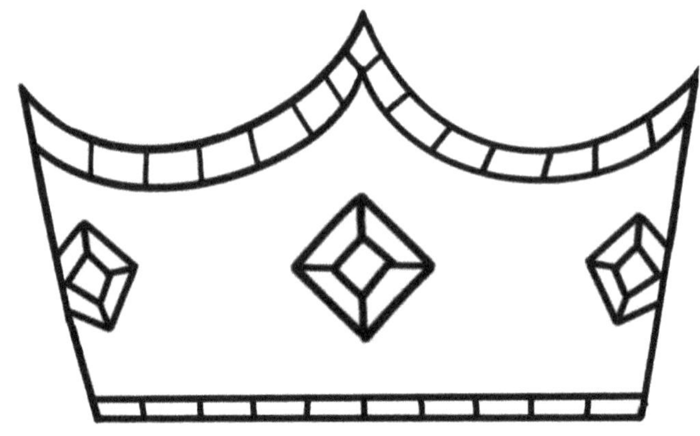

My crown is my power.

____

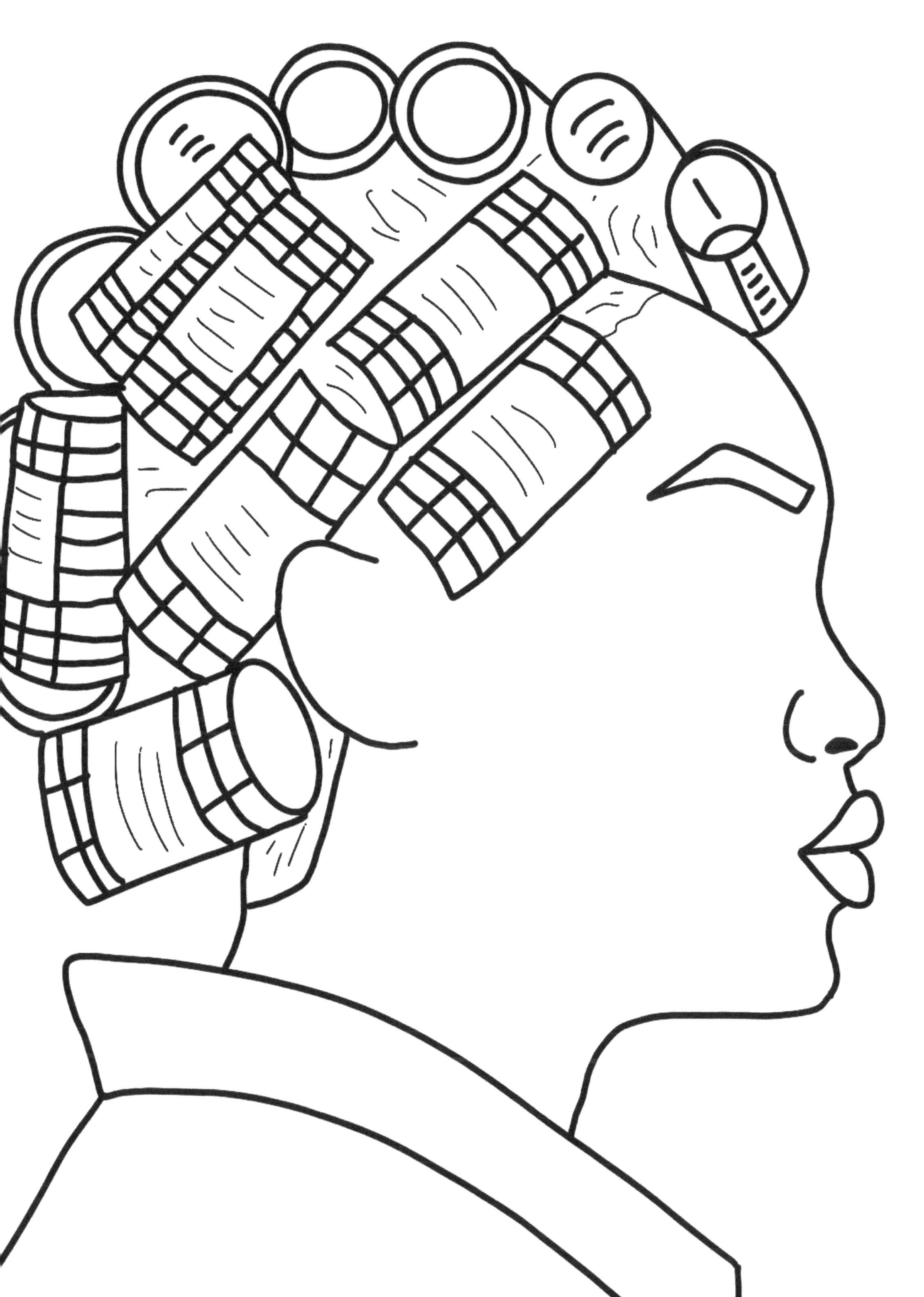

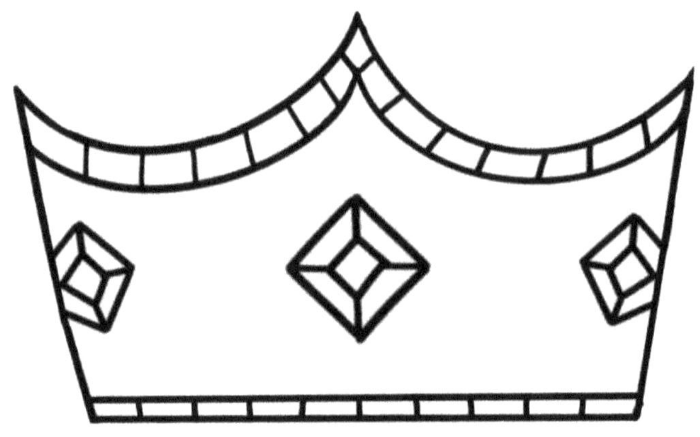

There is power in my crown therefore, there is power in me.

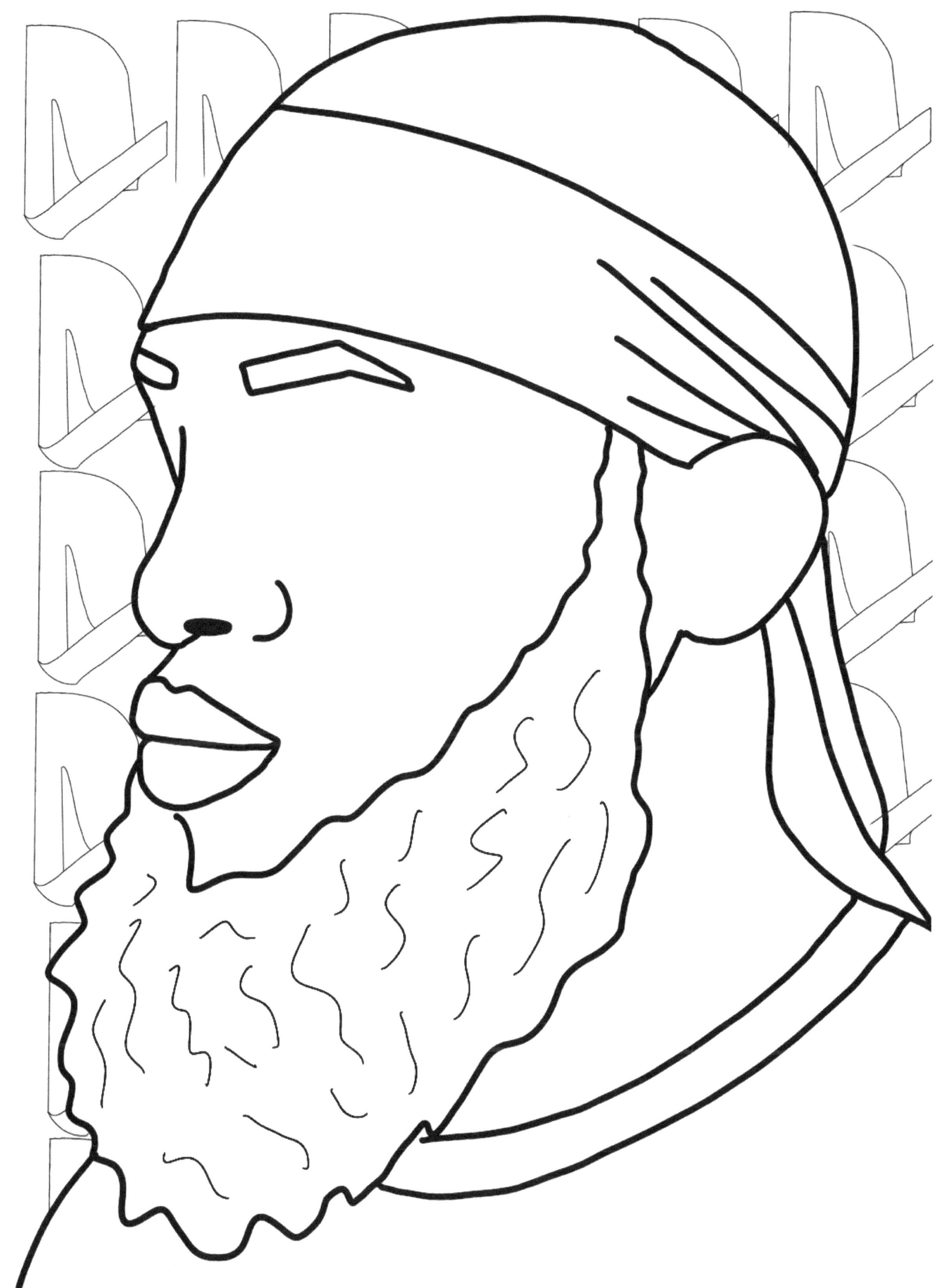

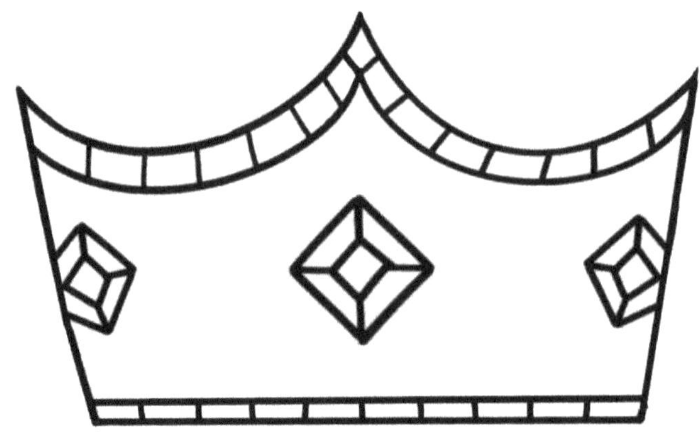

I don't have to change myself
to fit into what someone else
wants me to be.

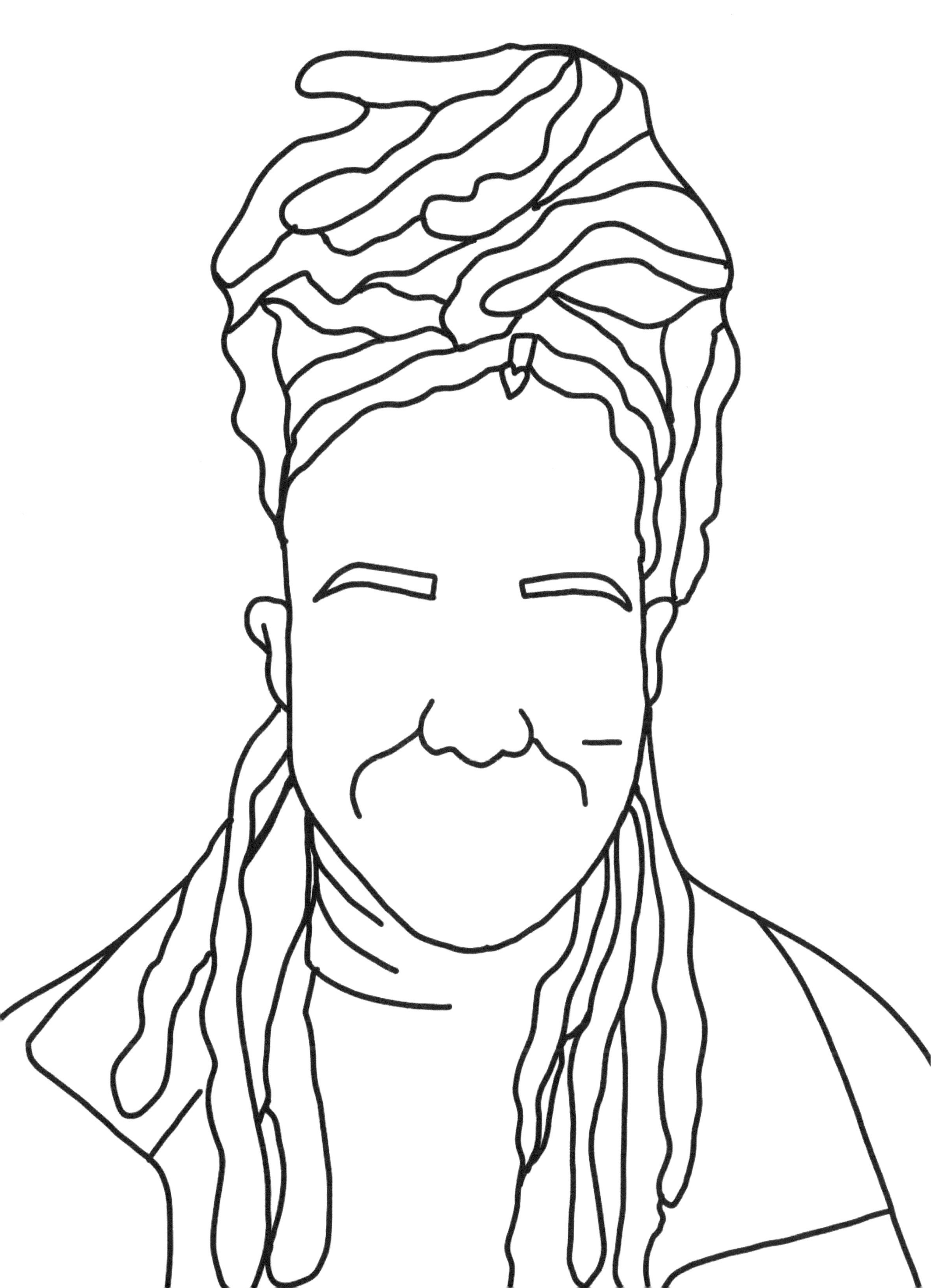

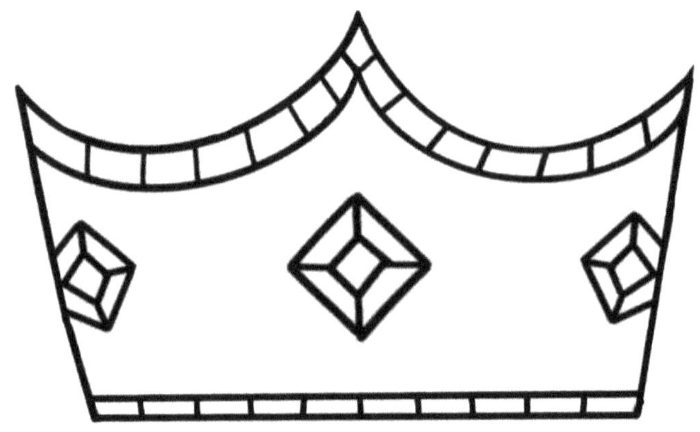

I am beautiful, confident, and loved just the way that I am.

____

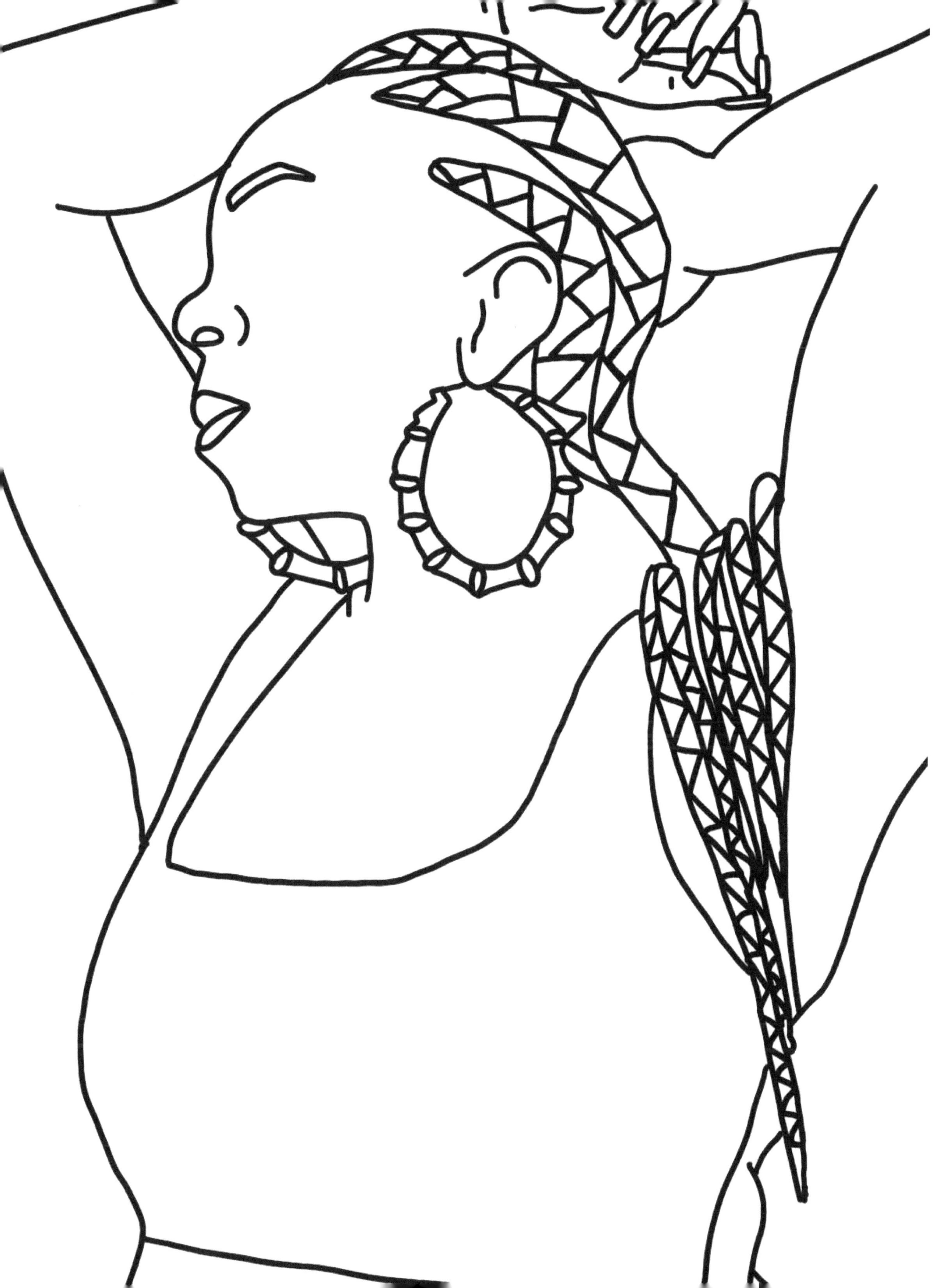

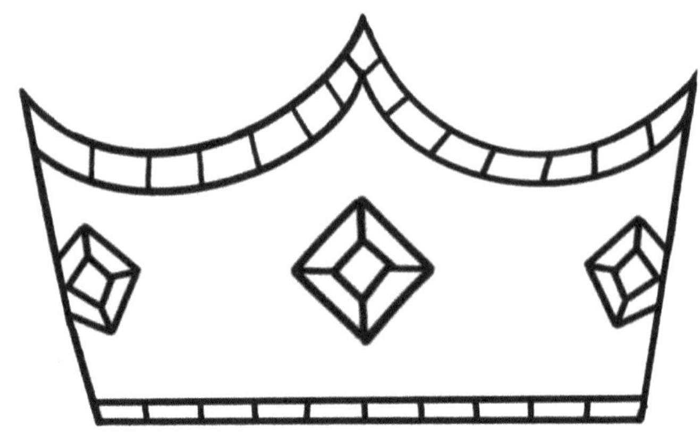

I have the power, autonomy, and authority to change my life with small daily acts of dedication.

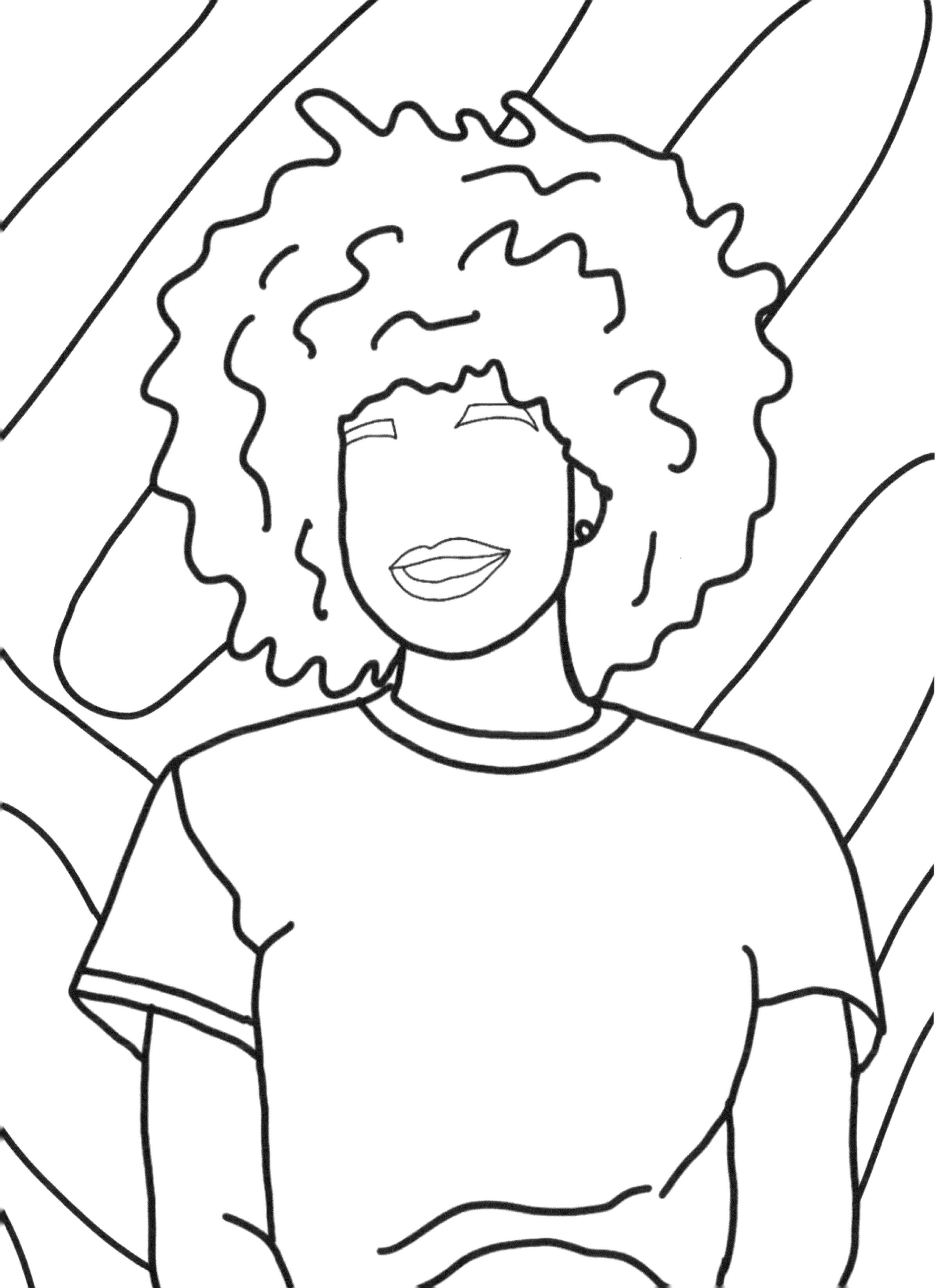

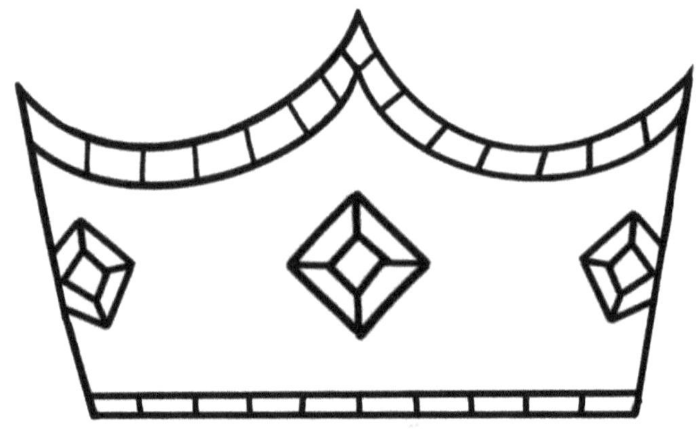

I look in the mirror and like what I see. I look inside myself and love who I am.

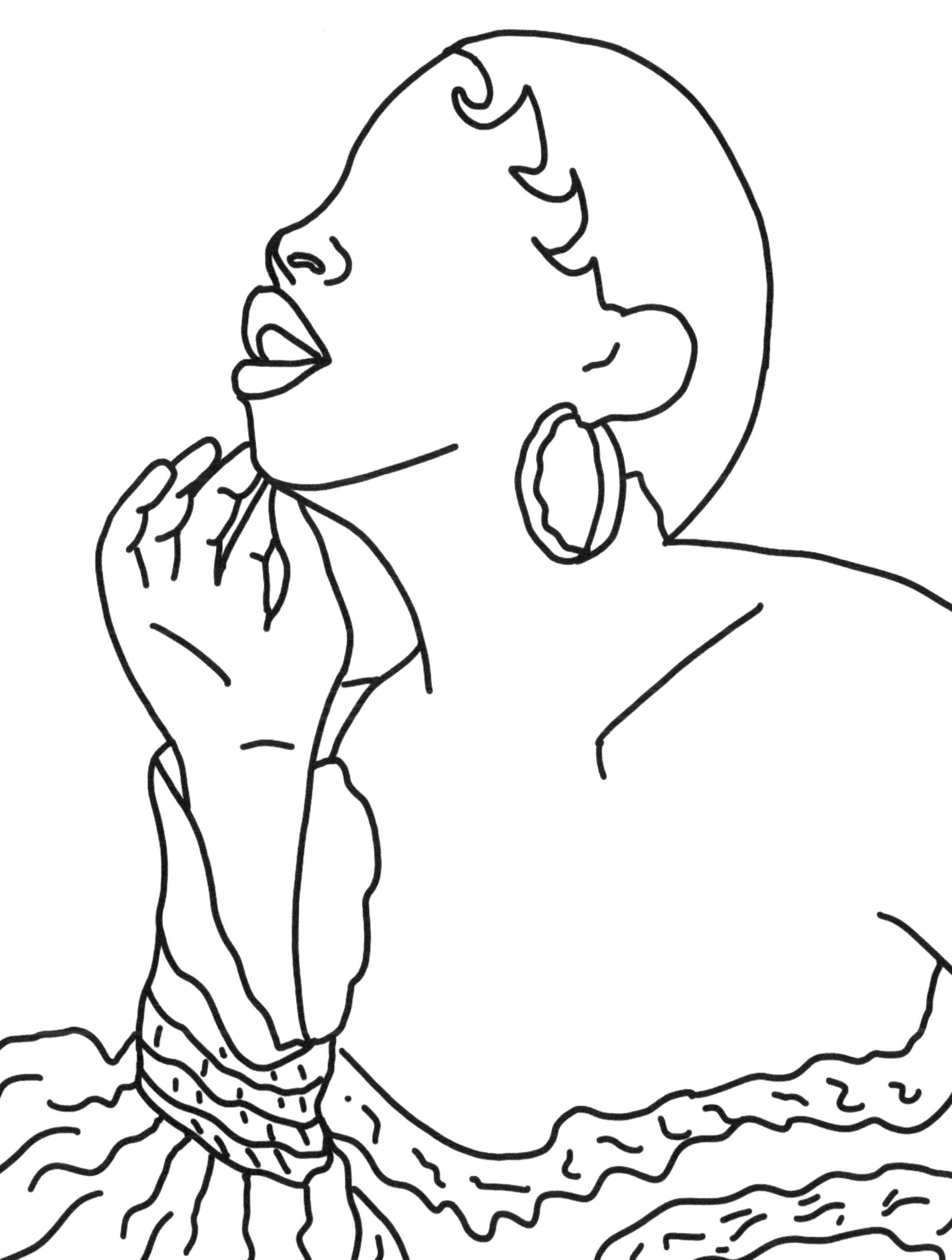

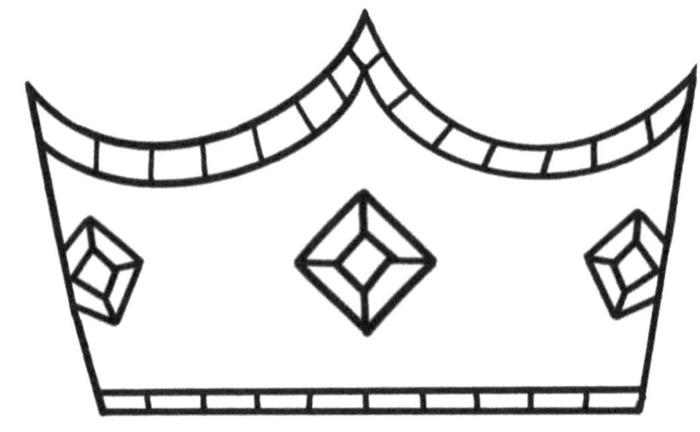

Even when other people don't like what I like, I know it is okay because everyone has their own opinion, but the one that matters the most is mine.

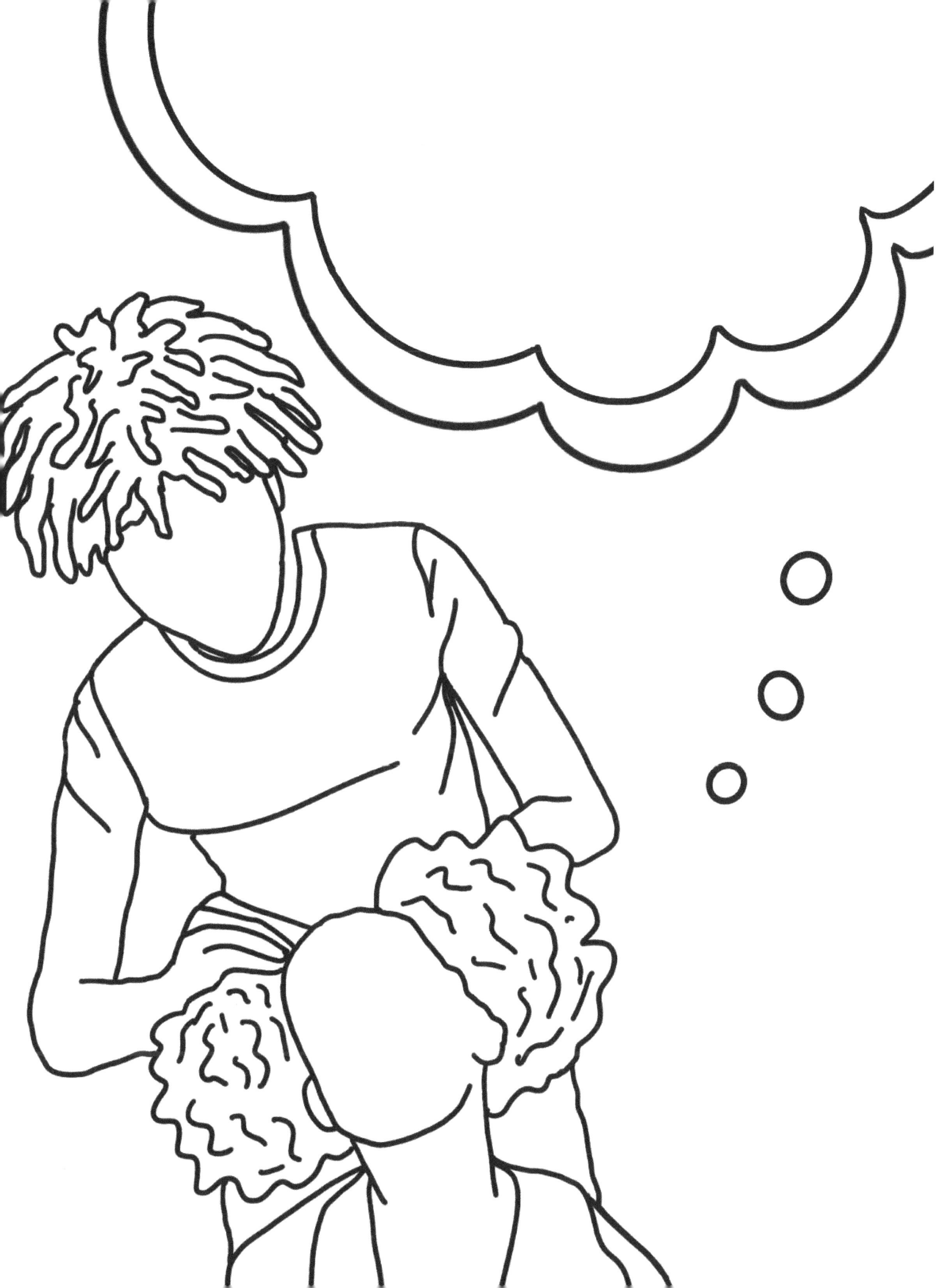

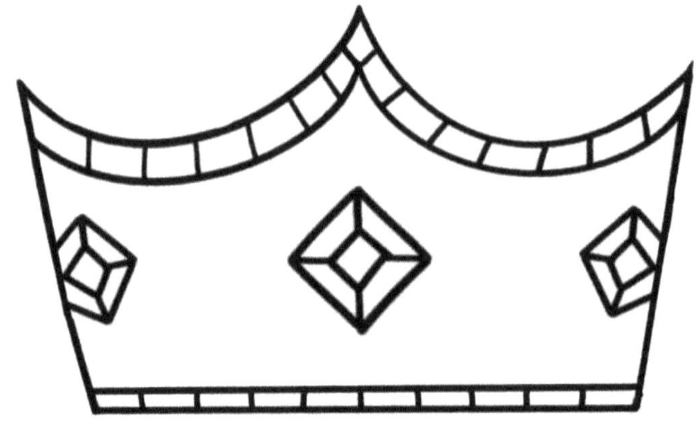

I am loved, adored, and
valued from the soles of my
feet to the tip of the crown
on my head.

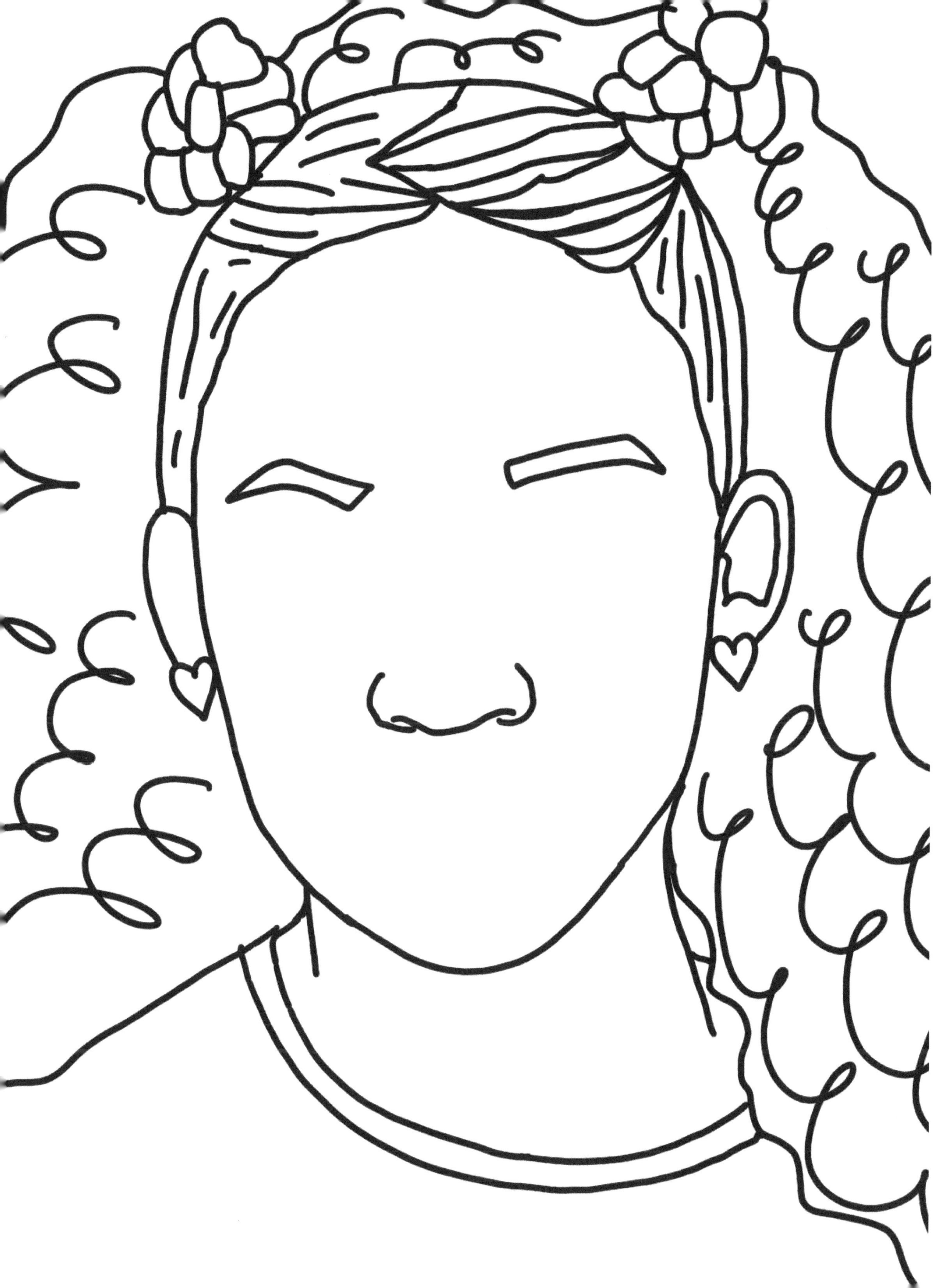

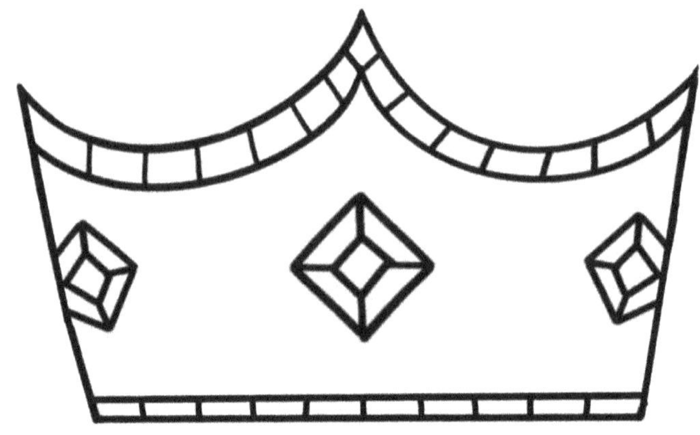

I love my hair.
My hair is my crown.

____

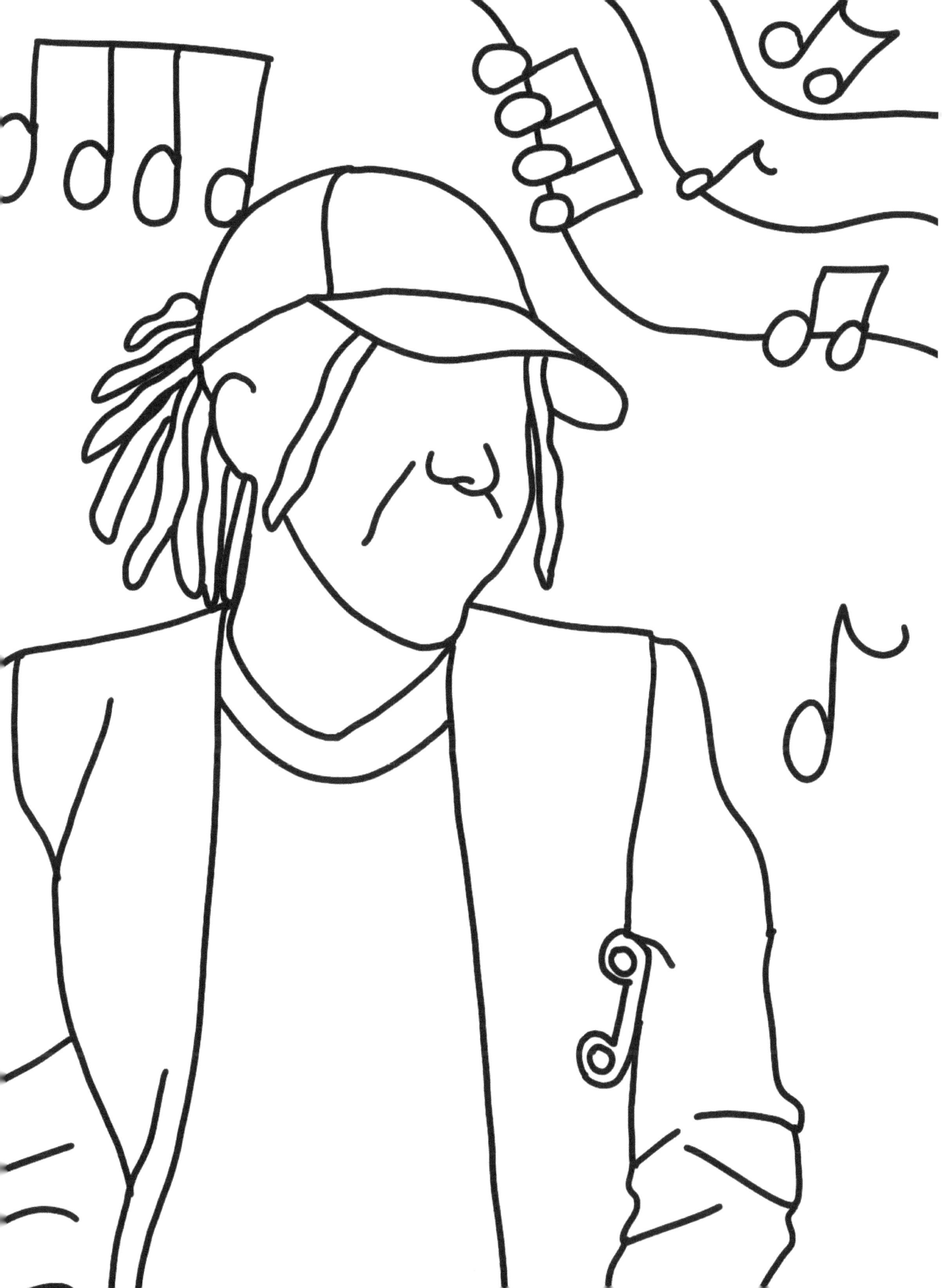

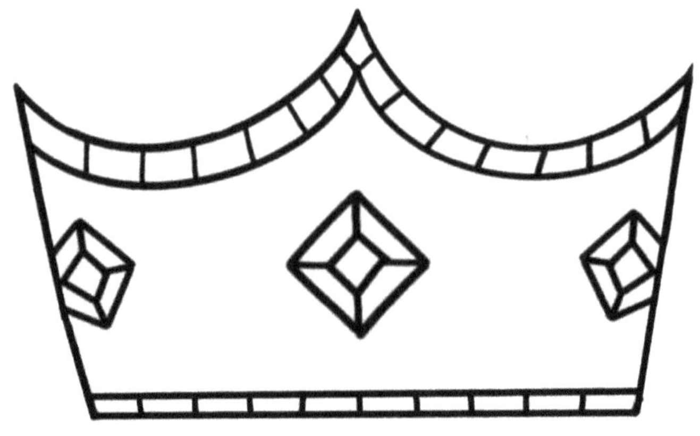

What is my favorite hair style for my crown?

____

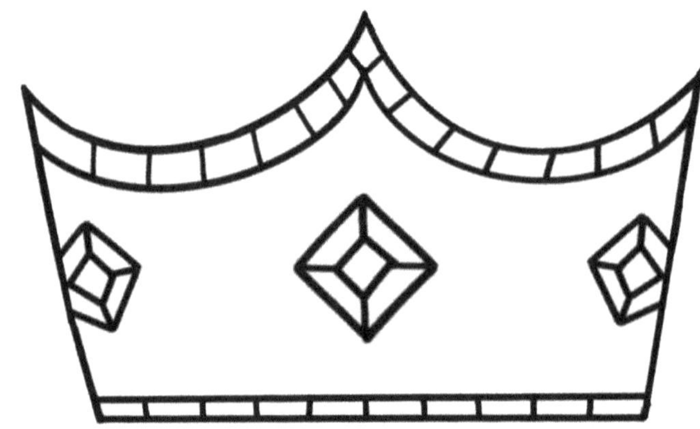

If you want advice on taking care of your hair or new styles, try searching for Youtube videos, Pinterest posts, and social media from your favorite Black content creators.

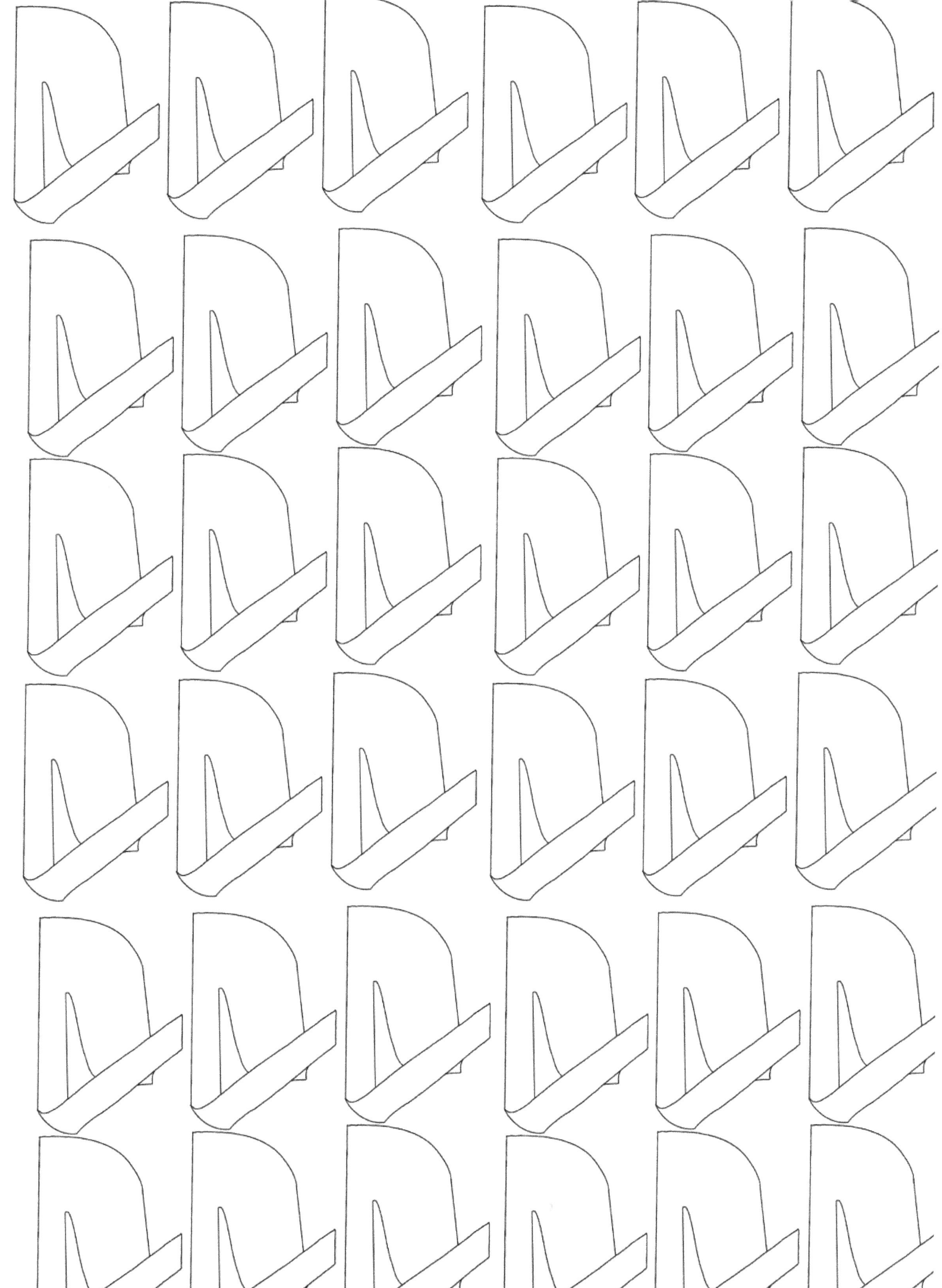

Whenever you feel insecure about your hair, whether that is how it grows naturally out of your head, if you tried something new, or if people are mean to you because of the way that your hair looks, remember that the crown that you have has been passed down through generations of people that look like you. It is okay to be unsure, but it is never okay to not be you. Be you in the best way that you know how and stay true to your wants, your likes, and your style.

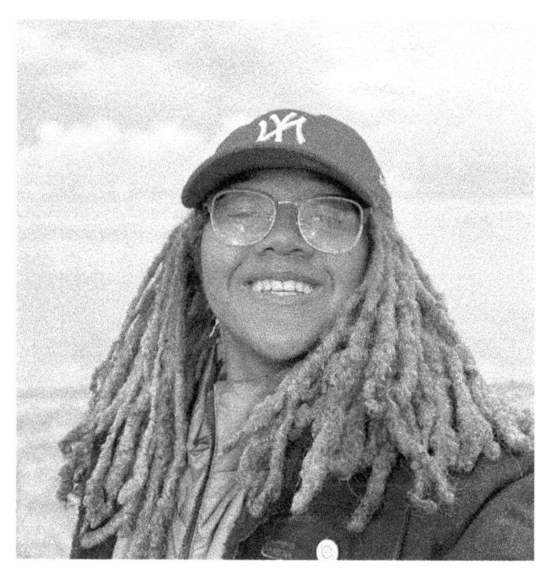

Creative Representation as a Movement for Change

Naomi Winston

There is nothing in life that is truly "permanent," especially when it comes to your crown. You can change your hair as much as you like and use it as a form of self-expression too!

This picture is right after I dyed my locs blond, and I was so nervous about it that I almost backed out of it. Do the things that scare you! Do it alone! Do it unsure! Do it no matter what other people think!

When you choose yourself, and yes, doing something as small or massive as changing your hair counts, you uncover a version of yourself that you never knew existed and unlock possibilities for yourself that you never thought possible.

It is okay to be unsure of your next decision in life, but remember, as long as you love the way that you look, the way that you dress, and your style, no one else's opinion matters.

Your crown only fits you for a reason, so wear it as only you can!

Remember, everything happens for a reason, and you are everything!

www.ingramcontent.com/pod-product-compliance
Lightning Source LLC
Chambersburg PA
CBHW040857070726
47599CB00035B/2028